Essays by Edward F. Fry and Donald P. Kuspit

Contributions by I. Michael Danoff,

Mary Jane Jacob and Paul Schimmel

Robert Morris   Works of the Eighties

Museum of Contemporary Art   Chicago, Illinois   •   Newport Harbor Art Museum   Newport Beach, California

This book is published in conjunction with the exhibition **Robert
Morris: Works of the Eighties** coorganized by Mary Jane Jacob,
Chief Curator at the Museum of Contemporary Art, and Paul
Schimmel, Chief Curator at the Newport Harbor Art Museum,
which was presented

February 14–April 13, 1986
Museum of Contemporary Art
237 East Ontario Street
Chicago, Illinois 60611

May 2–June 30, 1986
Newport Harbor Art Museum
850 San Clemente Drive
Newport Beach, California 92660

Edited by Sue Henger, Newport Harbor Art Museum
Printed and bound in Japan

Library of Congress Cataloging-in-Publication Data
Fry, Edward F.
    Robert Morris, works of the eighties.

    Bibliography: p.
    1. Morris, Robert, 1931-   Exhibitions.
I. Kuspit, Donald B. (Donald Burton), 1935-
II. Newport Harbor Art Museum. III. Title.
NB237.M63A4 1985   709'.2'4   85-25852
ISBN 0-917493-03-6

Cover illustration:
Untitled, 1983-84 (See cat. 17)
painted cast Hydrocal, watercolor
and pastel on paper
102 x 108 x 21 in.
(259 x 274.3 x 53.3 cm)
The Rivendell Collection,
New York

Contents

Edward F. Fry   5   Robert Morris in the 1980s

Donald B. Kuspit   13   The *Ars Moriendi* According to Robert Morris

    23   Catalog of the Exhibition

    64   Selected Exhibition History

    65   Selected Bibliography

    68   Lenders to the Exhibition

    69   Acknowledgments

    70   Trustees and Staff, Museum of Contemporary Art

    71   Trustees and Staff, Newport Harbor Art Museum

4

Figure 1
Enterprise (Burning Planet series), 1984
painted cast Hydrocal, oil on canvas, steel
141 x 148 x 60 in.
Photo courtesy Leo Castelli Gallery and Sonnabend Gallery, New York

Robert Morris in the 1980s

Robert Morris stands before us today as an undismissible presence that forces us to rethink the entire basis of modern American life, the entire history and ideology of American cultural and artistic modernism, and, not incidentally, his own role in that modernism...a role that now, suddenly, takes on a new meaning and coherence and which changes totally the way we understand both past and present.

Since the end of the 1970s Morris has made works which seem to reject every tenet that he supposedly espoused in, or contributed to, the situation of art from the early 1960s onward. His new works break with apparently every formal, esthetic concern and display what seems to be the inexcusably bad taste of celebrating death and morbidity: cenotaphs, skeletal reliefs and, more recently, the firestorms of nuclear holocaust. In his brilliant monumental works of 1984 Morris went even further in the direction of an apparently renegade loss of aesthetic faith by combining sculpture—the medium by which he has always been known—with painting and architecture into a new kind of composite art, culminating in such extraordinary achievements as *Enterprise* (fig. 1) and *The Astronomer*, which have no precedent in American modernism. Morris has thus apparently broken two taboos of the modernist faith at once: the integrity and purity of a given medium and the corruption of high art by literary and metaphorical intrusions from the outside worlds of politics, science, and power.

But Morris is not offering a personal version of *Apocalypse Now,* nor a backsliding, Turneresque version of the neosublime. His ambition here is of a higher and more encompassing degree, which one may initially identify as a radical, neomodern attempt to confront the tragic failure of the Protestant, American version of the Enlightenment. In doing so he addresses many levels simultaneously, ranging from the mental and technical domination of nature

and the fatal role of rationality, to the inability of American artistic modernism either to remain modern or to escape its self-imposed and self-sterilizing limits. His strategy is that of irony, raised to the intensity of the antisublime, an antisublimity that acknowledges the fatal seductiveness of apocalyptic sublimity, especially for the American mind, but which, somewhat like Terry Southern's *Dr. Strangelove,* dissolves that false sublimity by revealing another, authentic, and more awesome sublimity both in the universe itself and in human consciousness and will as they interact with the cosmos. To do justice, however, to the full scope of meaning and reference of Morris's art, it is essential to turn away from its immediate presence and to examine the underpinnings of the modern age itself.

The Tragedy of Enlightenment

The entire modern world, but America most of all, has evolved along lines first articulated by the eighteenth century Enlightenment but which had their beginnings far earlier. The Enlightenment's dethroning of tradition, precedent, aristocracy, and a theocratic and metaphysical framework for all of human activities was emancipatory, in every possible sense, for the ascending bourgeoisie: Careers open to talent; the autonomy of science, art, and law as parallel yet independent spheres of human activity, each with its own standards, logic of development, and consequently limitless potentiality for human betterment; and the resulting real progress of Western bourgeois societies in health, agriculture, transport, communication, the mass production of labor-saving devices, and the endless other fruits of a democratic, industrialized society in the process of "modernization."

So also, pure science, as opposed to applied, constantly expanded the knowledge and understanding of all aspects of the physical world, both through a mapping of facts and through theoretical generalizations for the ordering of those facts, leading hypothetically to a final limit at which the human mind would think and, in a sense, *be* the cosmos itself, thus drawing as close to the condition of an Omniscient Divinity as could be possible in a secularized and postmetaphysical age. But also, in a parallel action of Enlightenment, human intelligence explored man himself, both in his social dimension and in that presented by the human mind itself. Here, however, the possible limit conditions have proved to be more immediately elusive than those of the physical sciences, for the challenge in the second instance was the Kantian problem of the mind thinking itself, the limit condition being the mind becoming itself without losing awareness of itself. In the case of human society, the limit is the even less imaginable, because Omniscient, case of the human mind grasping all the possible interactions of all other minds, memories, and aspirations, and of specifying the possible social consequences of such an almost infinite universe of consciousness and volition. In the face of such overwhelming odds, it is no surprise that the endless unruliness and unpredictability of human societies provoked the invention of Utopias, extremist sects, and other supposedly rational principles of ordering and purification, all in the name of Enlightenment ideals—a temptation which has by no means come to an end in the twentieth century.

Such Faustian aspirations in all domains of human activity were central concerns of the Enlightenment-derived modern age. The dark side of the Enlightenment heritage—the payment of the Faustian contract—is nevertheless equally a part of the modern era, and is at least as prominent a feature as the disinterested search for knowledge. The dark side of the Enlightenment is that the bourgeois, secular quest for pure knowledge came to be a new principle of domination; the emancipatory promise of rationality turned into a nightmare of the loss of freedom without any compensatory transcendence remaining as consolation. This supreme irony underlying the entire modern age came about in two ways. Unwittingly, the autonomous, disinterested search for knowledge generated its own inner imperatives in every domain, opening an ever-increasing number of Pandora's boxes, each containing unforeseen consequences. Wittingly, the search for knowledge was translated at every new stage of discoveries into instrumentalized domination and control of both man and nature. This second, darker side of Enlightenment has overrun us with its onslaught: medical reduction of infant mortality generates runaway population levels, starvation, and war; better living through chemistry ends in all-encompassing pollution; the application of relativity theory and nuclear physics creates the pervasive nightmare of nuclear extinction at worst and the disposal of discarded nuclear fuels at best; psychological research is turned into the creation and manipulation of a mass public of passive consumers, if not pure ideological control as well; and the social and political sciences are just as easily converted into the tyranny of bureaucracies and of social engineering. In all these examples, as in the countless others endemic in the modern age, disinterested knowledge leads infallibly to the potentiality of its misuse, while the willfully instrumentalized application of both new and old knowledge becomes the technology of unfreedom. No Divine Intercessor hovers above this fray to save man from his follies, and few if any sons of the Enlightenment see fit, as their ancestors did on occasion, to dismantle or bury the dangerous secrets with which they trifle. The only metaphysics of the modern age is power, and in the Nietzschean struggle between disinterested knowledge and instrumentalized knowledge-become-power, power almost always wins, whether or not it is in the service of a noble cause.

This drama, which has been justly named the tragedy of the Enlightenment, rests ultimately on the process of secularization, from which arise all other Enlightenment principles: the enthronement of rationality; the abolition of historical tradition as a guide to conduct; the destruction of hierarchies of any kind; and the specialized immanence of the logic of progress in all domains, including the subsequent accreted histories of progress in these specialized domains and "disciplines." Secularization was the crucial enabling element which made possible both the disinterested pursuit of knowledge to any limit—the very essence of modernity—and the "modernized," instrumentalized use of such knowledge for the domination of nature and man. Secularization also removed any vestige of premodern theological or metaphysical constraints upon knowledge, most especially its conversion from truth to power. But there is a hidden historical dimension to the drama of Enlightenment which has survived the abandonment of tradition and which is also separate from the Enlightenment offspring of history-as-progress, be it linear and additive or a disjunctive sequence of paradigms. This hidden historical dimension is the persistence into the modern world of the pre-Enlightenment traditions of knowing the world theologically and metaphysically. Such premodern, substantive habits and traditions continued, in secularized guise, to provide an invisible yet determining framework for thought and knowledge within the overall project of Enlightenment modernity. It is thus within the metaphysical and theological traditions preceding the Enlightenment that a more specific aspect of modernity is to be found.

Although traditional, pre-Enlightenment Europe was Christian in its common acceptance of the hierarchies linking nature, body, mind, knowledge, memory, and the Godhead, there could not be a sharper division within that unity than between the Reformation and the Counter-Reformation, a division that grew even wider with the rise of post-Lutheran, Calvinist Protestantism, first in Europe and then in America. In the closed system of Counter-Reformation theology, all prior experience and all theological discourse were subsumed into an all-embracing symbolic syntax, hermetically sealed against any new experience that could not be assimilated to existing doctrinal structures. The partial secularization of such a metaphysics, in the form of a Cartesian, usually reductive, theory of knowledge based on mental a prioris, provided the underpinnings for French classicistic culture from the seventeenth century of Poussin and Versailles to the fully secularized, Enlightenment world of French nineteenth-century modernity.

In Reformation theology, however, a different metaphysics emerged, which led in three distinct steps to Protestant modernity. The first was the radical recasting of Catholic tradition in the Lutheran Reformation, which shifted the primacy of knowledge and salvation to the individual and to individual experience. The second step was Calvinist Protestantism and its intensification of the Lutheran focus upon the individual through the doctrine of predestination and the directly consequent belief in earthly prosperity as a prefiguration of salvation. In both the Lutheran and Calvinist stages of the Reformation, the direct, unmediated thoughts, experiences, and actions of the individual held a central position. But just as the Cartesian theory of knowledge marked a partial secularization of the Counter-Reformation, so also did Calvinist Protestantism signal a comparably partial secularization of Luther.

It is in the third stage of Reformation modernity—the secularization of pre-Enlightenment theology—that the double-edged nature of Enlightenment emerges most clearly, reaching both apotheosis and nadir in America, the most Protestant of nations. For Protestant modernity, the secularized, epistemological remnant of Calvinist theology, contains within it not only the primacy of the individual and of the individual's unmediated experience, but also two additional elements of the greatest consequence. The first is that the presecularized Calvinist doctrine of earthly prefiguration, when secularized fully, became an implicit cultural justification for the exploitation of both nature and man, as Max Weber's great thesis on Protestantism and capitalism convincingly argued. This exploitation, however, may also be understood as an inherent predisposition of secularized Protestantism to lower the threshold separating disinterested, substantive modernity and instrumentalized "modernization."

A second element, unique to secularized Calvinism, is a new, modern uncertainty in the relation between mind and body. In premodern Christianity, whether Protestant or Catholic, a hierarchy of mind over body was accepted as part of a more general, theological hierarchy: mind-body relations were understood to be mediated by a transcendental Christian framework that was firmly imbedded in both collective norms and individual memories. But in a modern, secularized world, the hierarchical relation between mind and body gradually receded and left behind an ambiguous mind-body dualism that was now also deprived of any mediating link. What remained in Protestant modernity was an unmediated parallelism of the individual's mental and bodily experience. This implicit theory or system of knowledge, as part of a secularized Calvinism in which the threshold between the substantive and the instrumental, the disinter-

ested and the dominating, is both weak and unstable, is the most general, historically derived foundation of American modernity in science, society, and art. In its substantive mode it is the basis for the empire of facts, for the priority of experience over theory, for law based on precedent rather than on analysis. In American art it encourages empirical realism, either in traditional techniques or by means of photography; and in American esthetic strategy it fosters the empirical borrowing of nonindigenous styles on the level of surface, formal appearances rather than according to intentions. When American modernity slips from substantiveness to instrumentalism, the consequences in applied science and the technological imperative are all too familiar. Equally familiar is the suborning of governmental and legal processes by lobbying and by bribery in its infinite disguises. American Protestant modernity retains its uncorrupted substantiveness only when it remains empirical, even if that empiricism involves the extension of human faculties by the most powerful of optical, mechanical, and electronic devices, and by the marshalling of ever more efficient means and deployment of ever larger computers for the amassing and sorting of scientific or sociological data. Yet of all the original ideals, explicit or implicit, of the Enlightenment, only the Kantian enterprise of the mind understanding itself provides the means by which the potential tragedy of the forces unleashed by the Enlightenment may be forestalled. Only if the consequences of the mind extending itself throughout the cosmos, as well as throughout the social order, are *re-presented* to the mind may the emancipatory potential of the Enlightenment be recuperated. Such a process may justly be called *modernism*: the self-conscious awareness of modernity, including the epistemological conditions bequeathed to that modernity by its premodern, theological past.

Robert Morris and American Modernism

This long theoretical digression may seem at first to be irrelevant to the issue at hand, the art of Robert Morris in the 1980s. Yet the instrumentalization of science, society, and art are the themes with which the artist has been struggling in these works. The issue of modern science run amok, corrupted, and enlisted in the service of domination leading to a potential nuclear holocaust, is so prominent a feature of Morris's recent work that it hardly needs to be singled out at this point. Less explicity obvious, however, is the way in which his engagement with this theme coincides, and is in fact linked, with the crisis of Protestant modernity in American art. An examination of the conditions of modernity and modernism in their esthetic mode will clarify this aspect of Morris's achievement.

If esthetic modernity implies the full exploration of the possibilities of art, including the possible logic of its development, then American Protestant modernity would focus upon the parallel empirical experiences of mind and body, unmediated by hierarchies or other premodern traditions. A condition of modernism—self-aware, self-conscious, and emancipatory—would then emerge when these cultural and epistemological conditions of modernity were re-presented in such a way that mind and consciousness, including bodily action and experience, understand their own workings. This self-understanding is thus emancipatory in the fullest sense and aspiration of the Enlightenment, since the previously active and determining conditions of mind and experience become accessible to the mind itself. In American esthetic modernity, this condition of self-understanding was first achieved in 1948 by Jackson Pollock. In his poured paintings, the empirical actions of the body and the equally empirical visual cognition of the mind are so intertwined and so nakedly stripped of representational functions that the result is a re-presentation to the self of the empiricism and unmediated mind-body dualism of Protestant modernity within which the self is located. Substantive esthetic modernity is thus revealed by the re-presentational strategy of modernism, creating a condition of supremely self-aware, self-liberating beingness, like the vision of the re-presented imagery of Pollock's own hands and body in *No. 1* of 1948: A limit case is attained in which the mind, within the autonomous category of art and in the context of a specific set of historical conditions, becomes itself by becoming aware of itself.

So powerful a moment of modernism has affected the entire subsequent history of American art, but Pollock's fusion of mind and body and his consequent revelation of the epistemology of Protestant modernity has never been reattained. Partial versions and approximations of it, rather than full modernism, have characterized subsequent American esthetic modernity. In particular, a schism has developed in American art since the 1950s between mental and bodily self-awareness, in which one or the other is explored but hardly ever simultaneously and never fused into Pollock's revelatory elimination of dualism. Thus mental re-cognition of familiar objects, as in Pop art, or verbal or mental self-referentiality, as in Conceptual art, have focused on one half of this dualism; and Minimal sculpture, environmental art, and dance performances have explored bodily self-awareness. Morris, however, is unique among all American artists since Pollock in his explorations of both the mental and the bodily, his ceaseless investigation of their interrelations, and thus his apparent awareness—his modernism—

at one or more levels of consciousness, of the epistemological tradition within which American modernity is situated.

The entire development of Morris's art becomes clear in this context. He began as a gestural abstract painter in the 1950s, often incorporating energized figural references in his paintings; he then, in common with an entire generation of American artists, reacted against painting. (One cannot help but wonder whether the young artists of that generation, upon reaching maturity, had an intuitive insight that the problem of modernism in painting had been solved before their time, and that the only territory open to a continuation of the discourse of modernity and modernism necessarily lay elsewhere. If this was in fact the case, it would be an esthetic prefiguration of Jurgen Habermas's later insistence on the modernity of communicative rationality.)

Morris's first extrapictorial preoccupations, at the beginning of the 1960s, were neo-Duchampian explorations of the phenomenal world of found objects, processes, systems, and their accompanying mental constructs. He then moved further into the experiential world of Minimal sculpture and its cognitive ambiguities, dance performances, and environmental art, all involving bodily self-awareness and its uncertain (because unmediated) relation to mental cognition and memory. This dialectical move from the virtuality of painting to its antithesis in the actuality of sculpture during the 1960s was followed by an expansion during the 1970s to Morris's deployment of distorting or misleading mirrors, labyrinths, and other situations requiring physical displacement in order to achieve perceptual and cognitive awareness. In some kinds of works, such as those involving mirrors, both bodily and mental/visual cognition were addressed simul-

taneously, but in such a way that their unmediated dualism, and even invented cultural norms and expectations serving as means to surmount that unmediated dualism, would be laid bare. In his labyrinths Morris addressed dualism with a second strategy of suppressing the mental and visual altogether, which by their absence would both generate bodily self-awareness and uncover the nature of mind-body dualism itself.

The *Blind Time* drawings of the 1970s offer an even clearer clue to Morris's attempt to uncover the epistemology of American art and culture, for in these drawings he explored the character of the relation between bodily action and nonvisual mental volition; as in the labyrinths, he eliminated visual-perceptual coordination, revealing the parallel but unmediated empiricisms in mind-body dualism; and he demonstrated, by means of its suppression, the role of empirical, corrective feedback between bodily action in the performance of a specific task and the simultaneous visual cognition of that action. To the extent that these drawings thus reveal the mind to itself, they generate a powerful, if partial, version of American modernism. Morris's work in the 1960s and 1970s is in fact one of the few examples since Pollock of a Kantian self-awareness of modernity. Rather than being "theatrical," Morris's art was a struggle to reattain modernism by means that confronted the epistemological issues underlying American modernity more directly and rigorously than those used by any painter and virtually any other artist of the period. The critical misunderstanding of Morris's "theatricality" by Michael Fried was also matched by a comparable misunderstanding of Pollock himself by Greenberg and his followers. The fact that Pollock's poured paintings are the record, the aftereffect, of what was originally a performance, a special kind of dance, was ignored in favor of the "presentness" of the result—a canvas that could be assimilated into the prior history of art visually and stylistically. This visual and stylistic empiricism was a remarkable instance of the unself-conscious methods of modernity being applied to the revelatory self-conscious conditions of modernism. Similarly, the promulgation of a post-Pollock, post-painterly abstraction through a supposedly self-critical purification of the medium of painting itself, as was attempted by Greenberg and his followers, was an example of the unself-conscious logic of progress within the autonomous category of esthetic modernity rather than an extension of Pollock's Protestant modernism.

The new direction in Morris's art at the end of the 1970s, which was incomprehensible to many observers, even those most sympathetic to his earlier work, began with the pivotal moment of his environmental installation of 1980, entitled *Study for a View From the Corner of Orion*. In this work three new elements surfaced simultaneously: a frame of reference that extends to the scale of the vastness of the universe; the theme of death in the use of real human skeletons suspended in mid-air in order to underline the nontranscendence of the human condition; and a conscious evocation of Bernini's Counter-Reformation religious orthodoxy (inverted by Morris's ironic antitranscendence), along with the baroque theme of infinite time and space.

This relatively sudden change in the focus of Morris's art, after almost twenty years of phenomenalist work dedicated to an extension of autonomous modernism, raises issues of the highest importance concerning the consequences of Enlightenment modernity in both science and art. In art, given that Pollock's achievement of modernism was to have a divided and partial continuity at

best and a relapse into modernity's unself-conscious logic of progress at worst, the prospects for human emancipation through autonomous art were rapidly dimming at the end of the 1970s, if not before. At the same time the American art world was also being rapidly instrumentalized through ever-expanding marketing and publicity operations; and art was itself becoming one more middle class career, with its paths for advancement and strategies for success and profit. Earlier attempts in the late 1960s and early 1970s by artists to achieve direct, emancipatory changes in society through nonesthetic actions had little or no lasting effects; and the use of art for political change at that time as well as subsequently had resulted in journalistic illustration or amateur propaganda imagery with little esthetic value or social effect. Thus, by the end of the 1970s, the situation of American modernism had reached a point of ineffectual (if not despairing) pointlessness, surrounded on all sides by a booming market for art that was naive, provincial and increasingly antimodern.

This crisis in esthetic modernism had already become long established in science. By the end of the 1970s it was all too clear that the Enlightenment mandate to understand all of nature, to think the universe with the human mind, had reached the point of a thoroughly corrupted, militarized instrumentalism which, coupled with the technological imperative, increased the likelihood of nuclear holocaust. The supreme irony of such a possibility is that the power of the mind to think and thereby become the universe could result in an explosive catastrophe that would inflict upon both the human mind and body the extreme of entropic violence which the mind has observed in nature. Mind becoming the universe would also participate in the entropy of the universe, and the self-reflexive

understanding of the mind as universe would coincide with entropic dissolution and death. Such a scientific modernism, at a limit condition of the mind as universe understanding itself only in the fraction of a second before entropy, would be a false, unwitting modernism, the tragic product of unself-conscious Enlightenment modernity and of its separation of human endeavor into autonomous but, in view of the consequences, vastly unequal categories. The darkest, innermost secret of apocalypse as unwitting modernism, however, is its seductiveness—not only as the temptation created by the technological imperative but also as the one sure means of surmounting the otherwise intolerable continuation of unmediated mind-body dualism in an ecstasy of simultaneous unity and release.

The enormous, almost insuperable task Morris has set before himself in his works of the 1980s is to confront the tragedy of Enlightenment modernity in both autonomous art and science, to break down the barriers separating the two so that the parallels between their respective estrangements from self-aware modernism will become evident, and to do so in such a way that an exhausted artistic modernism will be transformed and reemerge with a new emancipatory power. It is a measure of his ambition and achievement as an artist that he has come within reach of that goal in his recent works. In a long series of composite structures—part painting, part relief sculpture, part architectural frame/portal—he surrounds paintings derived from his *Firestorm* drawings with frames containing relief castings, in life size, of skulls, bodies, fetuses, sexual organs, brains, eyes, entrails, thrusting fists and phalluses of aggressive male will, flotsam and jetsam from all of Western life and culture. These frames, which developed out of Morris's *Hypnerotomachia* plaster reliefs, bend and contort as if under the most extreme forces imaginable, the detritus of earthly human existence being melded into an unspeakable flux, each element in the reliefs tinted with the glowing colors of the central firestorm. Just as these frames, molded by the artist's hands and body, are highlighted with the mental/visual attribute of color, so the images of the central firestorms are painted with his fingers: an interlocking complementarity of mind and body, unequally accented, coming together in painting and in relief, the parts inextricably juxtaposed physically and mentally within the unifying theme of apocalypse.

In the greatest of these works thus far, the regeneration of esthetic modernism by means of disruption and reformulation of the very foundations of Protestant modernity becomes so interlocked with the tragic hubris of Enlightenment science that the double nature of Morris's emancipatory neomodernism merges into a virtually inseparable whole, a wholeness comparable to that of Pollock's earlier modernism but now far more difficult to attain in a world incomparably more dangerous than the 1940s and bereft of those last shreds of innocence which still lingered in that earlier age. In *The Astronomer* of 1984 (fig. 1a), the human mind's eye, a barbed weapon like a feline phallus, thrusts with the speed of light into the cosmos to see and think its ultimate entropic secrets, consumed by the very firestorm it begets. In *Enterprise* (fig. 1), also of 1984 and, I believe, the greatest work until now in Morris's entire career, the firestorm spreads an ironic glow across the human detritus of its pulsating frame, watched by a Michelangelesque owl of death perched at the top; a structure of rods and spheres skirts the front of the work as a second ironic commentary on both applied physics and the vast folly of the organized enterprise of technology, the results of which it is now confronting.

Underlying all these unforgettable images and references is the brilliance of a second great dialectical act, comparable to Morris's original move in the early 1960s from the pictorial to the sculptural. In this second step Morris has synthesized the pictorialism of Pollock's achievement with the space-time phenomenalism of his own prior attempts to regain Pollock's original emancipatory modernism. The result is the fusion of painting and sculpture, of esthetics and the most tragic issue in real, nonesthetic life, and an almost coming together again of mind and body. The two touch, interlock, almost merge, as they would in the apocalyptic ecstasy of death, but the residual tension between them generates an all-important, neomodern awareness of the enormity of the dangers of modernity. This is an art that struggles to regain the lost wholeness of free beingness; it is a struggle to become modern again in the face of the decline of full, emancipatory self-awareness, be that decline the result of fatigue alone or of a willful embrace of new-old myths and their soothing amnesia. In the cultural history of the modern world, these works mark the emergence of a baroque Protestant modernism which subsumes all that preceded it into a new, fuller representation of a world torn by extreme opposing forces. Other, potentially even more catastrophic, consequences of human knowledge will undoubtedly follow our own, just as man will discover ever more violent forces in the cosmos itself. But works of art such as these stand alone in our present culture, unique in their embodiment of multiple levels of consciousness, knowledge, and meaning and in their presence as admonitory guardians of the idea of a possible free, fully human existence. For this philosophical and ultimately moral vision and for his ability to communicate that vision indelibly and unforgettably, Robert Morris deserves not only praise and gratitude but our most serious attention.

Edward F. Fry

Figure 1a
The Astronomer (Burning Planet series), 1984
painted cast Hydrocal, oil on
canvas, steel
114¼ x 190 x 31 in.
Photo courtesy Leo Castelli
Gallery and Sonnabend Gallery,
New York

1 *Untitled*, 1982
cast Hydrocal with metal frame
63 x 51 in. (160 x 129.5 cm)
Collection of Pamela and James
Heller, New York

The *Ars Moriendi* According to Robert Morris

*No one wept for the dead, because every one expected
death himself.*
Agnolo di Tura, Chronicle of Siena, *1348*

All autumn, the chafe and jar
of nuclear war;
we have talked our extinction to death…
Robert Lowell, Fall 1961

Robert Morris is the J. Robert Oppenheimer of modern art. Witnessing the first atomic explosion on July 16, 1945, Oppenheimer remembered a fragment from the Bhagavad Gita: "I am become Death, the destroyer of worlds." Morris returned in spirit to the moment of that explosion, through his monumental *Jornada del Muerto* (1981)—Journey of Death—titled after the place the first atomic weapon was tested. A wasteland, the primitive Jornada del Muerto seemed like the end of the world—an appropriate place for a nuclear explosion. Oppenheimer named the test site "Trinity," not after the Christian one, but after the Hindu Trinity of Brahma the Creator, Shiva the Destroyer, and Vishnu the Preserver. Trinity site in the Jornada del Muerto was a place to reflect on first and last things—where the creative and destructive, the human and cosmic, converged. The first atomic explosion, with its strange intellectual as well as physical beauty, was an apocalyptic event, inevitably evoking eschatological ideas.

Morris's death-predicated, nuclear disaster eighties works are his Trinity, his art's climactic "endgame," where he most physically and complexly articulates what his art was conceptually and subliminally about from its start—the indwelling of the nothingness of death in being. But his art has always been intensely physical, and these are not the first of his works to manifest death in their being—to serve as *memento mori* on a journey of death. Death's concreteness was his art's implicit subject matter from the start. Morris's Minimalist objects are the simple material forms of death, preparing for the process works using waste and smoke.

Oppenheimer seemed unaware of the existential implications of atomic power until the trauma of the actual atomic explosion. He believed he was on a disinterested voyage of intellectual discovery. Similarly, prior to his art's "refraction" of atomic power, Morris seemed to believe it was purely about art, testing its boundaries. Awareness of possible atomic catastrophe seemed to catalyze Morris to declare his death-orientation openly, making clear that his has always been an art of truth. As Georges Bataille wrote, "The servants of science have excluded human destiny from the world of truth, and the servants of art have renounced making a true world out of what an anxious destiny has caused them to bring forth."[1] The atomic explosion showed Oppenheimer that human destiny catches up with and is inseparable from science, and generated in Morris an anxiety about his destiny that led him to connect his art more explicitly than ever to the true world, if also, paradoxically, to make it more esthetic—"artful"—than it had ever been.

Morris's art is essentially applied theory. Both as intellectual and as administrator of his ideas, he has carefully controlled the adventure of his journey of death. The supposed randomness of his development is more apparent than real. Each "stylistic" change is another stopping place on his journey of death. Like cunning Odysseus's adventures, the seemingly bizarre artistic adventures that constitute the narrative of Morris's art can be understood as a series of willed accidents foreshadowing the climactic event he knows he will experience when he at last arrives home—when he at last will really die.

Oppenheimer gave death new means of dominance, demonstrating its omnipotence as never before. He let loose a new Black Death, releasing death's energy from the living atom. He knew that the atomic explosion was a cosmic demonstration—a potential destruction of the universe that recreated the moment of its physical creation—showing that the beginning and the end, the creative and the entropic, were one and the same.

Morris's art shares not only Oppenheimer's death-identification but also his cosmic perspective and obsession with power. The perspective turns the obsession into the paradoxical awareness that just when power is most explicit and triumphant it is most deadly, extinguishing itself and everything else. Morris's theatrical perspective existed long before the Hofmannsthal-like "World Theater" aspect of the eighties works—which allegorically deal with the crisis and disintegration of civilization as well as art, and which use a version of the traditional language of art to make a modern point about decadence. The Minimalist works are inherently "stagy" as are the various environmental (including his 1978 drawings on the prison theme) and mirror works, which in their different ways throw one into a seemingly illimitable space—literally outer and figuratively inner space. They converge in the 1974 *Labyrinth* (as well as some of the grand, labyrinthine mirror constructions), a theatrical rendition of quasi-infinite outer space; confined in and moving through it, one experiences quasi-infinite inner space. In general, the sense of the infinite and the theatrical are inseparable. Such works as the 1971 *Observatory* and the 1980 *View From A Corner of Orion (Night)* are explicitly cosmic in perspective. In his essay "Aligned With Nazca" he describes his experience of an "art" meant to be viewed from outer space—from the cosmos at large.[2]

The sense that art has played itself out and must become theatrical to preserve itself—its objects must become performance-like to have effect and meaning, carrying power and staying power[3]—has long been prevalent in Morris's oeuvre. He has always had a sense of the inherent entropy of art—even of art as a theatrical way of cultivating, as well as demonstrating, entropy. This is evident from his attempt to show the contradiction inherent in art by "introducing" into it "a kind of order...that is not an art order" and that

"maybe" makes [his] art "seem less like art than art was before."[4] This order implies the "non-hierarchic" character of modern art in contrast to traditional art's hierarchic character. Morris's awareness of entropy appears also in his half-serious, half-tongue-in-cheek announcement of modernism's death, in effect the ideological springboard for his "post-modernist" eighties works. His 1974 photographic self-portrait in "bondage" is an especially striking instance of Morris theatrically straddling the boundary between art and non-art. To speak of art as inherently theatrical means to understand it as the privileged realm in which the inextricability of such fundamental opposites is made manifest.

An emotional weariness with what underlies them [modernist forms] has occurred. I would suggest that the shift has occurred with the growing awareness of the more global threats to the existence of life itself. Whether this takes the form of instant nuclear detonation or a more leisurely extinction from a combination of exhaustion of resources and the pervasive, industrially based trashing of the planet, that sense of doom has gathered on the horizon of our perceptions and grows larger everyday. Concomitantly, credible political ideologies for the ideal future no longer exist and the general values underlying rationalist doctrines for an improved future through science and technology are crumbling fast....In any case the future no longer exists and a numbness in the face of a gigantic failure of imagination has set in. The Decorative is the apt mode for such a sensibility, being a response on the edge of numbness.[5]

This statement can be taken as both the esthetic and moral program for the *Burning Planet* works: their decorativeness articulates our numbness in the face of the threat of our extinction. Reconstituting the decorative by synthesizing

representational and abstract styles—a "confusing" synthesis, since both function allegorically as well as literally—the new works are presumably a gigantic success of imagination. Yet they too are haunted by the dichotomy between art and non-art which pervades Morris's oeuvre. They are art works that show how they are made as much as the *Box With the Sound of Its Own Making* (1961). That is, they have the same manufactured look. (As Morris says, much of his work, in its non-art aspect, refers to "an order of things pretty basic to how things have been made for a very very long time," that is, he "doesn't refer to past art but to manufactured objects."[6]) They establish a disintegrative kind of order that is not entirely an integrative art order. It is a nonhierarchic order in which no esthetic priorities can be determined. The *Burning Planet* and related works are structurally insecure. They have a peculiarly incomplete look, as though their parts had to be conceptually collaged to discover their unity. It is as though the work as a whole was anamorphic; its unity could be grasped only from a cosmic perspective. It is an unstable unity—a blind drift to unity rather than a realized togetherness of parts. Frame is as important as picture framed, and even when frame is incomplete (allegorically "broken," like Barnett Newman's *Broken Obelisk*) or more than one kind of frame is used—or the central picture itself is fragmented, as occurs in several works—each part is as important as every other. No part of the work is privileged over any other, not even the black felt which plays a cameo role in one work, a self-quotation reminding us of an earlier stage in Morris's development as well as the "gravity" of his theme. All parts loosely relate, sometimes through an ambiguous congruity, usually through an informal metonymic/metaphoric connection. While each element that Morris uses—socialized sign or primal mark—can be understood as irreducible or generic, their unity is not preconceived—

predetermined. Relation is not guaranteed or predictable. This is typical of a construction or assemblage. Assemblage's uncertain unity perfectly suits the sense of coimplication of frame and picture, matter and energy, death and power.

Morris's eighties works are subtly dissonant assemblages of fragments that generally hang together, but their particularity—and imaginative success—lies in their vigorous assertion of their "fault lines." Part of the works' power is in these fractures. They subvert the works' general tendency to be decorative, or rather, give it a different slant: disrupting the glamorous numbness of the decorative, the fractures make self-evident the extinction or nothingness the decorative mediates—the living death (numbness) the decorative asserts yet obscures. T.W. Adorno's conception of what makes for success in a modern work of art springs to mind: "the criterion of success is twofold: first, works of art must be able to integrate materials and details into their immanent law of form; and, second, they must not try to erase the fractures left by the process of integration, preserving instead in the aesthetic whole the traces of those elements that resist integration."[7] In Morris's nuclear extinction works there is no one immanent law of form, making their disintegrative potential more radical, their fractures more substantive. As much as anything else in the work, they "gesturally" pantomime the destructive power of the nuclear explosion. In these works it is generally the central image of the explosive, smoky firestorm that resists integration with the frame, with its signs of doom, or death and power—skull and bones and dead fetuses, and phalluses and phallic fists (opposites that do not smoothly integrate). Even when there is a show of integration—usually by establishing an erratic continuity between tongues of smoky flame (picture) and grotesquely long fingers of death or long-stemmed flowers

of life (life and death forces are typically con-fused in Morris's frame)—there is a fresh demonstration of fragmentation. For example, when the death's-head leaves the frame and invades the the picture, or when figures, more or less in disintegrative process of metamorphosis, appear in the central picture.

Conflict, the major mode in which disintegration displays itself, is everywhere in these works, giving them their creative/destructive drive and sensual, pleasurable texture— their obscene beauty. Morris has lifted the taboo on sensuality that seemed to exist in his early works, although it can be argued that their epistemological preoccupation with the concrete was a sublimated sensuality. The new sensuality is not unrelated to the fact that the works reify conflict, conceiving it as a kind of perverse harmony. In the extinction works Morris shows himself to be an exemplary hypermodernist. Adorno has written:

> The taboo on sensuality in the end spreads even to the opposite of pleasure, i.e., dissonance, because, through its specific negation of the pleasant, dissonance preserves the moment of pleasure, if only as a distant echo. The hyper-modern response is to be wary of dissonance because of its proximity to consonance. Hyper-modernism…prefers to join forces with reified consciousness rather than stay on the side of an ideology of illusory humanness. Dissonance thus congeals into an indifferent material, a new kind of immediacy without memory trace of its past, without feeling, without an essence.[8]

Adorno has articulated the paradox of Morris's development. Through the sixties and seventies he explores the dissonance between art and non-art—including the spectator as non-art eager to identify with art. (In the distorting mirror works, the spectator is identified by art, that is, distorted so

as to become "art"—remade into its order.) Sensuality is generated by the ambiguous, difficult relationship between these opposites. With the eighties work, sensuality seems to return with a vengeance, but it is a sham sensuality. For it is the sensuality of extinction—a sensual presentation of Nothingness in which there is not the slightest illusion of humanness. Death brings with it a false consciousness of eroticism, much as eroticism brings with it a false consciousness of death. The extinction works articulate "a new kind of immediacy without memory trace of the past." The debris that clutters the frames is more ideological than memorable; the death's-head under whose auspices all occurs is eternal. The extinction works are really "without feeling, without an essence"—without authentic sensuality which signals the human.

This is why it is a serious mistake to regard Morris's colors as Turneresque or his fluidity in general—especially on the frames—as art nouveau, or the works in general as baroque. For these signal a residually sentimental, "humanistic" relationship to nature, in Friedrich Schiller's sense of sentimentality as restoring a lost relationship with an idealized nature. The atomic truth makes that impossible, for it gives us nature not in the sentimentalized/humanized form of the picturesque (as Turner, art nouveau, and the baroque do), but as a transhuman—inhuman—reality. Morris shows us this reality determining the human microcosm, which appears vividly if also pedantically—semantically—on the frames. (They have "human appeal" by reason of their illustrative character, accessibility as "message.") It also determines the indifferent, inhuman macrocosm, that is, the central image's firestorm, which is readable as an omen but incomprehensible in itself. The extinction works articulate nature as Pascal understood it, "an infinite sphere, whose center is everywhere and whose circumference is nowhere."

The works' forceful center centrifugally erupts through the rectilinear frame, belying the perception that it is a boundary that contains anything. Morris's works, by reason of their articulation of the infinite let loose by nuclear extinction, are clearly sublime, offering "the counter-image of mere life."

Morris is not so much "hyperallusive" as sublime—which is to be beyond style. His art does not so much "gamely" or opportunistically manipulate styles as pose the general problem of the conflict between the process of esthetic reconciliation which style is and the process of insistent concretization which reality is. Morris reconciles every known style with every other by showing that all exist on the same esthetic continuum, freeing himself to attend to the riddle of the ambiguous reconciliation of art with reality, restated in particularly dramatic form in the extinction works. They expose this conflict, central to art—showing it to be inherently a dialectic of the sublime—as perhaps never before in Morris's art. Adorno has written that "the ascendance of the sublime is identical with the need for art to avoid 'playing down' its fundamental contradictions but to bring them out instead. No longer is reconciliation the result of conflict; the only aesthetic purpose is to articulate this conflict."[9] As Annette Michelson has argued, Morris, like Richard Wagner and John Cage, "attacks, through a process of distension, the notion of wholly separable formal modes," "extending the transgressive tactics of the *Gesamtkunstwerk*" to "a reflective limit at which the very notion of Composition is reversed."[10] Michelson has connected this sublime decomposition—"deconstruction"—to Morris's aspiration to "a concreteness, an immediacy of presence greater than any purely linguistic concept would seem to afford."[11] But it is clear that Morris's obsession with the "very concrete" or "very much there"[12]—entropically concentrated matter—is

contingent upon his equally deep obsession with concrete nothingness, the very much not there. It is through a process of extinction that Morris arrives at the concrete. Only when it is experienced as irreconcilable with the process of negation that brought it into being can the concrete be said to be affirmed.

Morris, then, conceives of art-making as a kind of *Ars Moriendi*. The demonstration of the non-art within art, or their inextricability, shows that in a sense art is living death. To make art today is to experience its death. But Morris's art-making—exemplarily in his eighties extinction works—is an art of dying in a deeper sense. The *Ars Moriendi* was a popular booklet (1564–70), almost half illustrations. Morris's eighties extinction works, from the *Firestorm* series (1982), form an *Ars Moriendi* and show his art seeking a new publicness and substantiveness. Like it, they combine text and image and are generally apocalyptically oriented. They are not unrelated to Albrecht Dürer's high art treatment of the Apocalypse, which draws on the populist *Ars Moriendi*. And like it, they deal with the dying person's mental state. If, at the moment of death, one was in a state of sin—filled with anger, impatience, or avarice—one's soul was jeopardized for all eternity. The state of sin was one of resistance to inevitable death.

The Gita also deals with one's spiritual state at impending death, advocating that it be a state of Yoga-like "indifference," "casting off attachment" (2:48). The Gita is a dialogue between Lord Krishna and Prince Arjuna, who is about to begin a battle and face destruction. Lord Krishna is Arjuna's charioteer, in effect showing him "the way," instructing him in the attitude with which he must face and endure death. One must be "moodless." The purpose of the extinction works is to lead us to "the Rule of Meditation"

on the changeless. Such meditation alone is the path to indifference or godlike detachment.

Morris, no longer the mortifier of the flesh of art he was in his Minimalist phase, uses his knowledge and power of making to create works which, by confronting us with extinction in emblematic form, put us in a position to follow the Rule of Meditation. In the extinction works Morris plays the role of Arjuna learning the Rule—attaining a "contemplative" attitude to face the nuclear war that will result in the extinction of humanity. In other works, such as the *Jornada del Muerto* and the *Firestorm* series, Morris deals with actual events of World War II—the firestorms which arose from the saturation bombing of Dresden and the atomic bombing of Hiroshima—which presage the final nuclear firestorm, fabulous in scale and import. Indifference meets—masks?—futility in Morris's eschatological eighties works. Indifference, a state in which salvation is possible, is barely differentiated from futility, a state of sin. As with Oppenheimer in the Jornada del Muerto, Morris is in effect fighting for his soul's eternal future.

To paraphrase Schiller, "the more imperious the subject matter the greater the artist's need to subsume it within an order of his own making."[13] Morris's extinction works demonstrate that death truly considered—the death triumphant in the total war inseparable from the use of nuclear weapons—is so imperious a subject matter that it cannot help but make any order created by the artist to subsume it seem inadequate. Morris's nuclear extinction works are *necessarily* fragmented—their differentiation into two- and three-dimensional parts is a sign of their domination by death. Such fragmentation suggests their transience; it is not simply an indication of intellectual deconstruction but of potential literal destruction.

Continuing Schiller's line of thought, Morris's "constructive sense of freedom," which should show itself in "his articulation of the subject's latent structure, and [which] would include his fluency and the way he prevented the interest of any one part disrupting that of the whole," puts him in a paradoxical position. For to depict death is to depict disintegration—that is its "latent structure." Morris's extinction works are extraordinary in their fluency; this comes from their articulation of disruptive disintegration as smooth integration. Such fluency is the result of a marvelous engineering tact. (Morris studied engineering in college; his "self-deconstructing" constructions can be regarded as showing his ingenious engineering abilities, as well as climactic realizations of the Constructivist ideal of the work of art as an engineering project.) Despite the works' obviously fragmentary character, there is a quasi-holistic aspect to them, especially in the firestorm's depiction. Morris's brilliant articulation of the unity of disintegration and integration—destruction and creation—makes his works powerful communicative actions, for it indicates that he understands the "simultaneity" of system and lifeworld.

There is ample evidence that Morris was death-obsessed from the beginning of his career. It sometimes seems as though he intended to joke death out of coming for him—preempting it, as it were. In 1965 Barbara Rose described Morris's project for his own mausoleum:

> It is to consist of a sealed aluminum tube three miles long, inside which he wishes to be put, housed in an iron coffin suspended from pulleys. Every three months, the position of the coffin is to be changed by an attendant who will move along the outside of the tube holding a magnet. On a gravel walk leading to the entrance are swooning maidens, carved in marble in the style of Canova.[14]

The same opposition exists in the extinction works but in subtler form. "Carved" sentimental frame is juxtaposed with fiery picture, coldly rendered.

The ironical, tragicomic mausoleum project shows Morris's typical narcissistic grandiosity. It can also be understood to show how profoundly he experienced the thought of death. It always had cosmic majesty for him. The cosmic or oceanic experience—which Morris's *Burning Planet* works articulate with an anguished flair—has been understood by Freud as a symbolic return to the womb, the place of one's creation. Can the oceanic experience be understood as a "pre-experience"—rehearsal—of death, rather than a restoration of birth? Both involve a return to an undifferentiated state, in death's case through entropic dedifferentiation. Death is as "melting" or orgasmic an experience as love, which may in part explain the phallic imagery in many of the extinction works.

It is worth noting that the 1974 self-portrait poster (fig. 2) presents an image of fettered power and has a sadomasochistic dimension to it, as does the equally notorious *I-Box* (1962), in which Morris also appears "nakedly." Many of Morris's works—the labyrinths and distorting mirrors, and even the Minimalist and process works—establish a sadomasochistic relationship with the participant observer, or put him in a sadomasochistic situation. Anthony Storr regards sadomasochism as "pseudo-sex," for it is "an expression of the status struggle," that is, the power struggle—the struggle to be master rather than slave, to dominate rather than submit.[15] (This struggle is inherent in theater, which is why it is the art which most explicitly shows what art is about. In theater the artist attempts to dominate the spectator by sadomasochistically "submitting" to—simultaneously dominating and enslaving—him.) (See fig. 2a.) "Phallic envy" in both sexes indicates desire for power in "the domi-

nance hierarchy," a drive whose "price...is to be excluded from the pleasures of love."[16] The climax of Morris's pursuit of the pleasure of power is his extinction works, whose cold sensuality has nothing to do with love.

In any case, Morris's mausoleum project shows his acute awareness of the body. He has spoken of the body as "in some way a measure of the work...the fact of the work reflecting back to the body, its scale, and that in turn reflecting the scale of the work back to the person." Perhaps the most scandalous work in which Morris represented his body is the *I-Box*. It can also be understood as having to do with death. Morris, as naked as on the day he was born—as naked as one will appear before God—is fitted in what might be called a conceptual coffin, in the shape of the letter "I." Like certain monks, Morris shows himself living in his coffin. His identity is entombed in his image, and his image is entombed in the "indifferent" linguistic self that belongs to everyone, but that can also be understood as changeless, unlike the mortal body it contains.

Morris's cenotaph works (1979–80) continue, in concept and assemblage structure (fig. 3), the narcissistic death-preoccupation as well as the projected grand scale of the mausoleum proposal. They also have the same jaunty, joking manner as the *I-Box* and self-portrait poster, and much of Morris's writing[17] and work. It is certainly apparent in the distorting mirrors and labyrinths, which comically trap one. I would argue that this ironical manner is an immature form of the Indifference the Gita teaches—a kind of manufactured demonstration of the Rule of Meditation. It almost seems to be daring death to strike him down—as, I think, the arrogant poses of the *I-Box* and the self-portrait poster do. Indeed, one can understand the latter—note the military helmet—as a perverse image of Arjuna in battle dress.

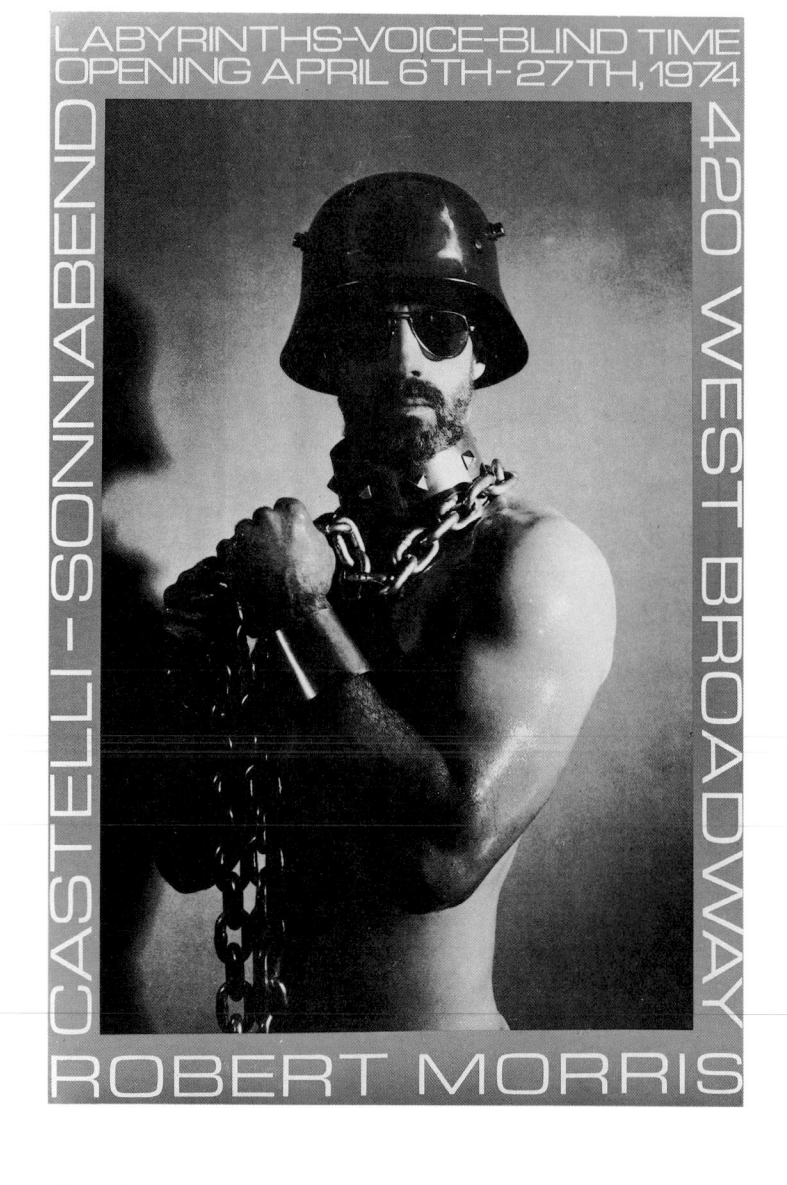

Figure 2
Poster for Castelli-Sonnabend
Gallery Exhibition,
6-27 April, 1974
36⅞ x 23¼ in.
Edition of 250
Photo Courtesy Leo Castelli
Gallery, New York

Figure 2a
Costume for Theater
Performance, *War*, a
collaboration of Robert
Morris and Robert Huot.
Performed at Judson Church,
New York City, Spring 1963.

The three *Blind Time* series (1973 and 1985, which Morris drew blindfolded; 1976, drawn by a blind person directed by Morris) also seem particularly telling demonstrations of the critical role entropy plays in art and art-making. The artist does not necessarily know what he is doing—what "insight" he has—when he is making art. Working blindly undermines the traditional idealization of the artist as someone who can "see through" everything as well as see everything clearly. It is deliberately entropic; the artist puts himself in the precarious position of being the critical spectator of his own art. He puts himself inside and outside it simultaneously, in an ambiguous creative/destructive relationship to it. Paul de Man observes that it is because the critic is "in the grip" of a "peculiar blindness" that he is perceptive, insightful. His "language could grope toward a certain degree of insight only because [his] method remained oblivious to the perception of this insight. The insight exists for a reader [spectator] in the privileged position of being able to observe the blindness as a phenomenon in its own right—the question of his own blindness being one which he is by definition incompetent to ask—and so being able to distinguish between statement and meaning."[21]

In the *Blind Time* drawings, vertigo is ceaseless, as in the nuclear extinction works. Are the *Blind Time* and *Firestorm* drawings statements or meanings? Are they—this question can be asked not only of the *Burning Planet* works, but of Morris's entire oeuvre—language or truth?

I contend that Morris's entropic art, and his general conception of art as inherently entropic, exists to catalyze, as well as function as the esthetic correlate of, the "freedom" of Indifference advocated in the Gita. Michael Podro has pointed out that Kant's esthetics presented a new conception of the freedom that art affords, created by combining the two traditional meanings of artistic freedom. "The construc-

tive procedure of the artist, the first sense of freedom, was conceived as bringing about the second, an inner composure. And in this way the role of art was seen as overcoming our ordinary relations to the world."[22] Morris uses the "constructive," engineered entropy of art—reflecting the destructive entropic processes ("blindness," war) of the world—to achieve "destructive" entropy, that is, the constructive attitude of Indifference to the destructive world. In this way, art overcomes our ordinary attitude to the world, while still participating in it. Art comes to be a way of accepting human destiny.

Rudolf Arnheim writes that "the increase of entropy is due to two quite different kinds of effect; on the one hand, a striving toward simplicity…and, on the other hand, disorderly destruction. Both lead to tension reduction."[23] Both operate in Morris. The "anonymous" (Indifferent) Minimalist works are perfect examples of the increase of entropy through simplicity. For Arnheim, the tension reduction achieved by "a minimal structure at a low level of order" can, "in the extreme…reach the emptiness of homogeneity."

Morris's Minimalist sculptures never reached the emptiness of homogeneity, for they incorporated the heterogeneity generated by the spectator's, or their own, movement. Thus, the simple L-shape structures Morris exhibited in 1965–67 can be moved. This displacement, however minimal, was sufficiently "anabolic"—Arnheim's word—to establish what he calls "a [minimal] structural theme." Such a "theme represents what the work 'is about,'" and functions as a "countertendency" to entropy, for it "introduces and maintains tension." Morris's Minimalist sculpture, including the felt pieces, is tendentiously antithematic (this can be argued for the *Burning Planet* works as well, simply by their idolization of extinction), yet the physical tension in it implies a

need for an increase in entropy to bring it under complete "control." While the *Burning Planet* works assert entropic Indifference in the face of a countertendency to "content," tensing content presents itself as the anxiety-arousing historical possibility of nuclear disaster the works articulate. Entropy is paradoxical. At the same time that it makes the works antiutopian, it makes them antihistorical. But it also presents emotional extinction (Indifference, nonattachment) as a kind of utopia, and vigorously asserts the violence and tensions of history. This ambiguity is still another demonstration of the art/non-art dialectic that makes the extinction works, and Morris's art in general, "expressive," if hardly empathic.

The eighties works also increase entropy by creating an effect of "disorderly destruction." The Promethean cosmic fire stolen from the gods is catastrophically burning out of control in human history. Morris's art is explosively charged with the discontents of both divine art and human civilization.

As Michelson has noted, Morris is an essentially philosophical artist. He is a more profound philosopher than even she recognized—a "true philosopher," for he "is ever pursuing death and dying" (Plato, *Phaedo*, 64A). For Plato, the body is "a hinderer of acquirement of knowledge." Is Morris more of a Platonist than is realized? His obsession with the body is countered by his attempt to increase the entropy in his works to the limit. Simplicity gives the illusion of preservation, but it is destructive. The material of Morris's works seems to promise the immaterial. The *Burning Planet* series "promote" dematerialization, disembodiment—the catastrophe of human substance turning to insubstantial shadow, as occurred on the Miyuki Bridge in Hiroshima, drawn as part of *Jornada del Muerto*. If Morris's art is about death and its

Figure 3
Preludes (for A.B.) (detail)
Roller Disco: Cenotaph for a Public Figure, 1979–80
Italian onyx, silkscreened text, light, metal, plastic installed with black paint; onyx: c. 35 x 34 x 7 in.
Courtesy Sonnabend Gallery and Leo Castelli Gallery, New York

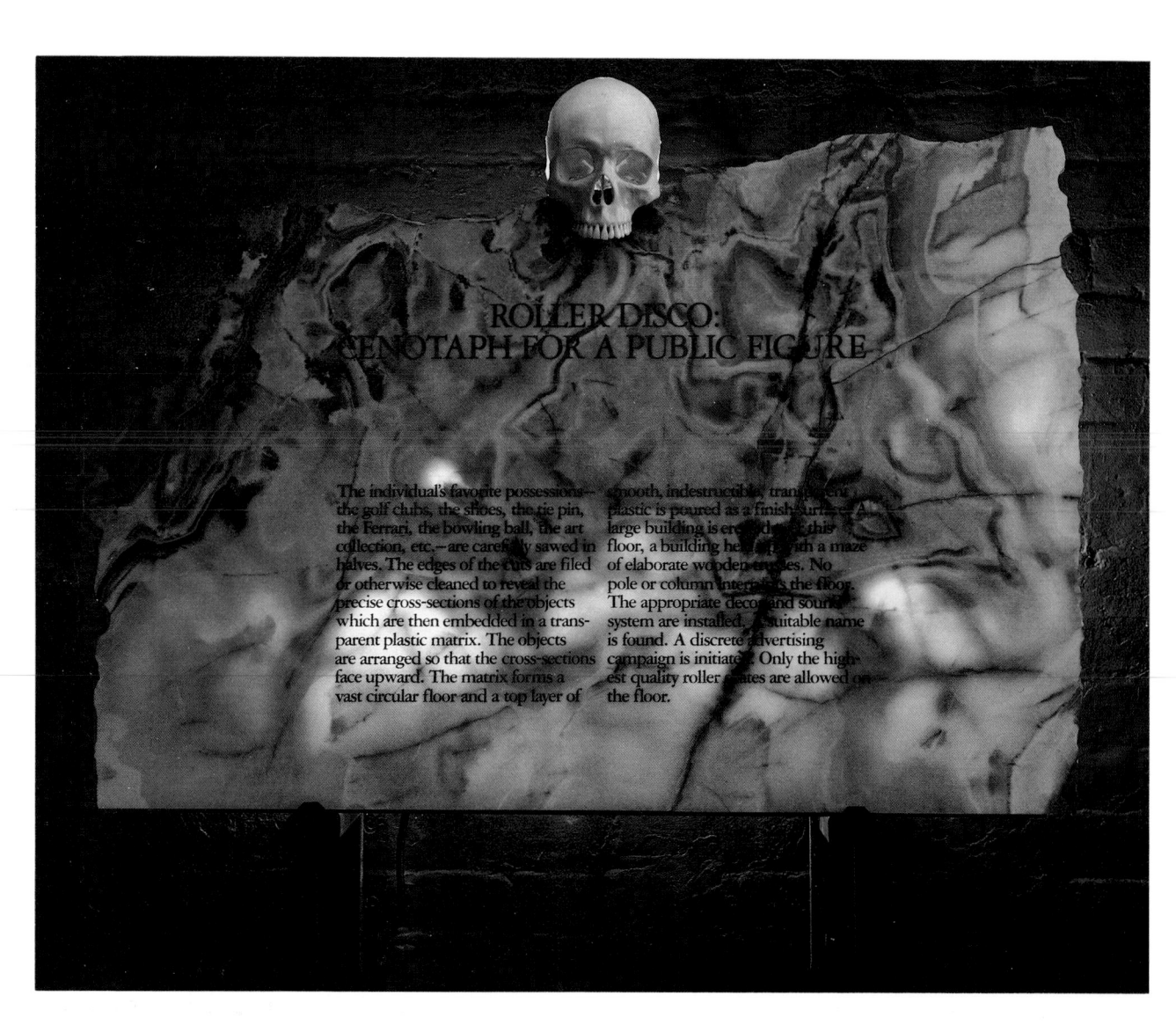

ROLLER DISCO:
CENOTAPH FOR A PUBLIC FIGURE

The individual's favorite possessions— the golf clubs, the shoes, the tie pin, the Ferrari, the bowling ball, the art collection, etc.—are carefully sawed in halves. The edges of the cuts are filed or otherwise cleaned to reveal the precise cross-sections of the objects which are then embedded in a transparent plastic matrix. The objects are arranged so that the cross-sections face upward. The matrix forms a vast circular floor and a top layer of smooth, indestructible, transparent plastic is poured as a finish surface. A large building is erected over this floor, a building hexagonal with a maze of elaborate wooden trusses. No pole or column interrupts the floor. The appropriate decor and sound system are installed. A suitable name is found. A discrete advertising campaign is initiated. Only the highest quality roller skates are allowed on the floor.

entropic effect, one has to reexamine the status of the body, and of bodiliness in general, in his art.

A. E. Taylor has pointed out that "it is...a mistake to attribute to Plato, as is so often done, the definition of philosophy as 'meditation on death.'" The Greek word Plato uses "does not mean meditation but *rehearsal*...the repeated practice by which we prepare ourselves for a performance.... The thought is thus that 'death' is like a play for which the philosopher's life has been a daily rehearsal. His business is to be perfect in his part when the curtain goes up....It is implied throughout the argument that 'philosophy' has the special sense...of devotion to science as a way *to the salvation of the soul.*" [24] Again, theater rears its head. Morris's reliefs are a performance of death. The Indifference they catalyze is necessary if the philosopher is to be perfect in his part when he faces death. Morris, who understands the "science" of his art very well, and whose work in general is inseparable from a kind of scientific understanding of the properties of materials and landscape, and who is an eternal actor, may or may not save his soul in the coming nuclear extinction. But he has positioned it in the drama of death he has unfolded so that it seems changeless.

Donald B. Kuspit

Notes

[1] Georges Bataille, "The Sorcerer's Apprentice," *Visions of Excess, Selected Writings, 1927-1939* (Minneapolis: University of Minnesota Press, 1985), p. 225.

[2] Robert Morris, "Aligned With Nazca," *Artforum,* 14 (Oct. 1975);26f. Many of Morris's works imply the same "cosmic" or aerial perspective—a grandiosity of spatial layout. This includes the various "splay pieces" of 1967–69, as I call them, including the different untitled metal and wood beam pieces, as well as the felt pieces, *Earthwork* (1968), *Steam Cloud* (1969), and various associated untitled pieces. In a sense, the mirror pieces also imply a cosmic perspective, in that they seem to expand space limitlessly and illusorily—the basic condition for the existence of the sublime.

[3] I am suggesting that Morris, wittingly or unwittingly, reconciles the false bifurcation of "Art and Objecthood" (theater) posited by Michael Fried (*Minimal Art: A Critical Anthology,* ed. Gregory Battcock [New York: E. P. Dutton, 1968], pp. 116–47).

[4] Robert Morris, "A Duologue" (with David Sylvester), *Robert Morris* (London, Tate Gallery, 1971; exhibition catalogue), p. 16. Morris's sense of the self-contradictoriness of the art work by reason of the "paradox" of its being at once art and non-art shows that he is an "unhappy consciousness" in Hegel's sense. For Morris, the "merely contradictory being" of art, its "inwardly disrupted," "dual-natured" character, is its true nature. G. W. F. Hegel, *Phenomenology of Spirit* (Oxford: Oxford University Press, 1977), p. 126. This accords well with the generally skeptical nature of his art, for the unhappy consciousness is a "stoical" hypostatization of skepticism.

[5] Robert Morris, "American Quartet," *Art in America,* 67 (Dec. 1981):105.

[6] Morris, "A Duologue," p. 16.

[7] T. W. Adorno, *Aesthetic Theory* (London: Routledge & Kegan Paul, 1984), pp. 9–10.

[8] Adorno, p. 22.

[9] Adorno, pp. 281–82.

[10] Annette Michelson, *Robert Morris* (Washington: D.C., Corcoran Gallery of Art, 1969; exhibition catalogue), p. 23. Michelson notes that for Morris the characteristic *Gesamtkunstwerk* "passage from the scenic space of Theatre to the landscape space of the Theater of Operations, lies through a Theatre of Consciousness whose dimensions are articulated by structures perceived in time" (p. 27). The nuclear extinction works are the most ambitious demonstrations of such a passage. It involves at once "the radically engaging physicality" of the work, its power "to question the aesthetic...distinction ...between a 'real' or operational space—that of the beholder—and a 'virtual' space, self-enclosed, optical, assumed to be that of sculpture" (p. 35).

[11] Michelson, p.9.

[12] Robert Morris, "Dance," *The Village Voice,* Feb. 3, 1966, p. 24.

[13] Michael Podro, *The Critical Historians of Art* (New Haven: Yale University Press, 1982), p. 6.

[14] Barbara Rose, "ABC Art," *Minimal Art: A Critical Anthology* (New York: E. P. Dutton, 1968), p. 295.

[15] Anthony Storr, *Human Destructiveness* (New York: Basic Books, 1972), p. 62.

[16] Storr, p. 69.

[17] For example, in "The Art of Existence: Three Extra-Visual Artists: Works in Progress," *Artforum* (Jan. 1971), Morris invents fictional figures who are disguised versions of himself. "American Quartet" concludes with a disclaimer that subverts the argument, if headlining its dialectical character. The whole Duchampian aspect of Morris (Michelson, pp. 50–53), can be understood not only as a tour de force of modernist irony subverting meaning—or fetishizing meaninglessness—but as an example of American high jinks humor, not always as black as h₄s been thought.

[18] Storr, p. 62.

[19] Robert Smithson, "Entropy and the New Monuments," *The Writings of Robert Smithson* (New York: New York University Press), pp. 9–18.

[20] Rose, p. 296.

[21] Paul de Man, "The Rhetoric of Blindness," *Blindness and Insight* (Minneapolis: University of Minnesota Press, 1983), p. 106.

[22] Podro, p. 6.

[23] Rudolf Arnheim, *Entropy and Art* (Berkeley: University of California Press, 1971), p. 52.

[24] Quoted in Jacques Choron, *Death and Western Thought* (New York: Collier Books, 1973), p. 50.

Catalog of the Exhibition

Contributors
IMD   I. Michael Danoff
MJJ   Mary Jane Jacob
 PS   Paul Schimmel

In the dimensions of the works, height
precedes width and width precedes depth.

1   See page 12.

2   *Untitled*, 1982
    cast Hydrocal with metal frame
    69 x 111 in. (175.3 x 406.4 cm)
    Courtesy Sonnabend Gallery and
    Leo Castelli Gallery, New York

Robert Morris's first Hydrocal works, made in 1982, fall some-
where between shallow relief sculptures and thickly impastoed
paintings. These objects were made by the artist's pressing
things into plaster and then casting the result in Hydrocal,
reversing the negative impressions into positive reliefs. Because
they are white and human anatomy is featured, they suggest
ancient friezes. But because the anatomy is body parts rather
than entire torsos and the arrangement seems by chance, these
works also suggest the fossilized record of a great disaster. Morris uses images of human debris to convey a vision of chaos:
skulls, brains, torsos, feet, fists, phalluses, bones, and teeth
tumble about in a maelstrom of apocalyptic devastation.

The title, *Hypnerotomachia*, was suggested by Francesco
Colonna's *Hypnerotomachia Poliphili*, an Italian prose romance
published in 1499 and accompanied by 172 woodcuts. The title
is a Greek neologism translated as, "The Strife of Love in a
Dream." The romance deals with the recovery of past values,
alchemy, the destruction of edifices, dismemberment of bodies,
and the loss of love found in a dream. Thus, the book may be
seen as an analog to the kinds of concerns Morris demonstrates
throughout the works in this exhibition.

The pictorial aspect of these works surprises, since Morris is
best known for the abstract, three-dimensional art he developed
in the 1960s. However, Morris believes that by the late 1960s,
abstract art was in the process of disintegrating. And by the
beginning of the 1980s, Morris was focusing on concerns that
readily lent themselves to a pictorial format. In 1981 he wrote:
"a sense of doom has gathered on the horizon of our perceptions and grows everyday"; it is linked to "returning nightmares
of nuclear war."

Specific aspects of the subject matter of the *Hypnerotomachia* are foreshadowed by, for example, the *Five War Memorials*
of 1970 and the eight cenotaphs with skulls of 1980. Actually,
the reliefs continue major interests that Morris has evolved in
the past 25 years: the basic nature of things, the process by
which we know them, the process by which they come into
being, the process of annihilation.

In these white reliefs there is a strong sense of process. Paradoxically, action is stopped and yet there is a perception of

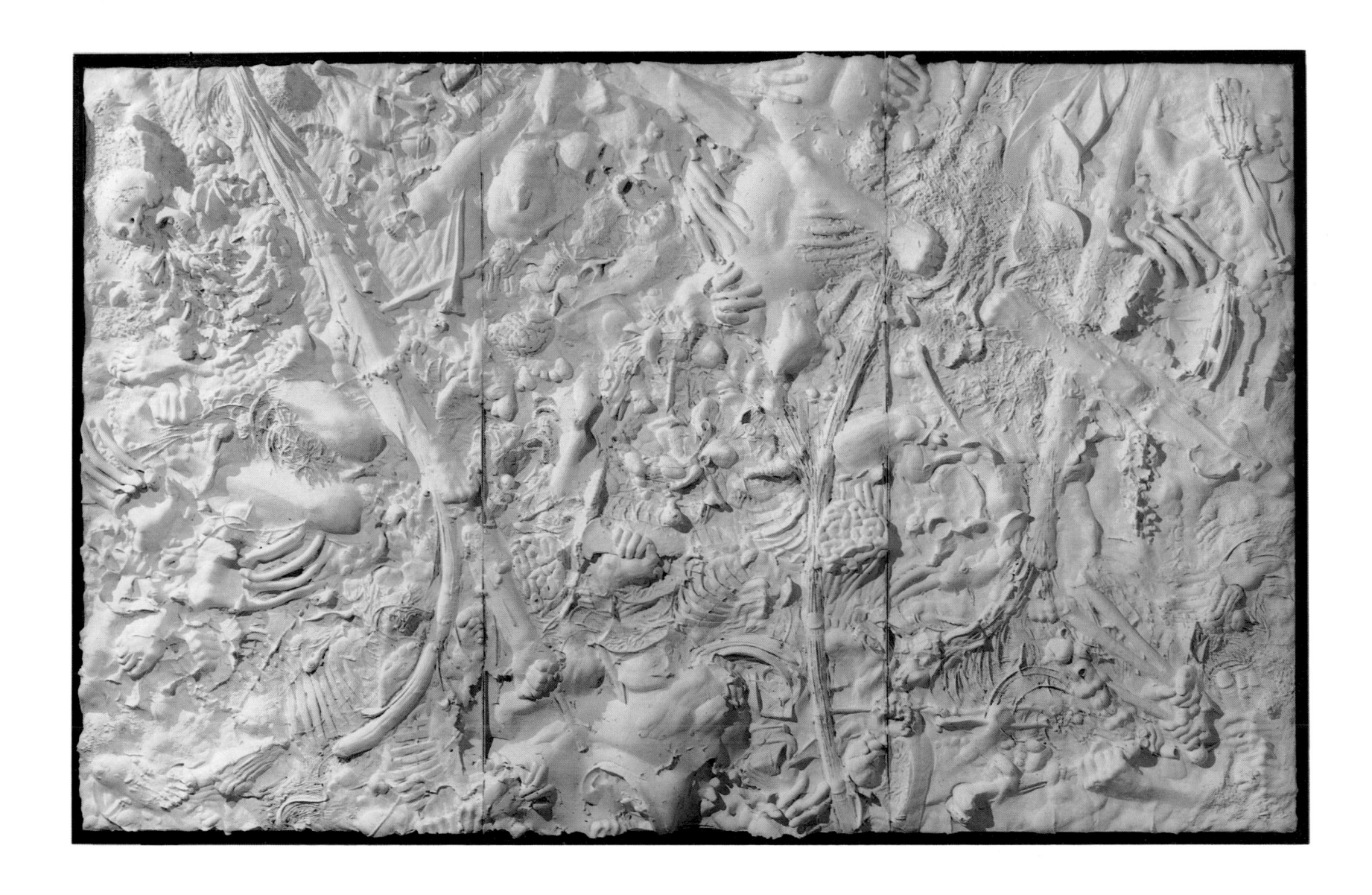

3   *Untitled*, 1982
cast Hydrocal with metal frame
63 x 87 in. (160 x 221 cm)
Collection of Martin Sklar,
New York

movement and the passage of time. Multiple fists and forearms power their way through the image. Fingers trace paths through the medium of their depiction. In these works Morris has effectively responded to the ancient challenge of narrative art: finding a convincing way to suggest motion in a medium that is static.

Process has long interested Morris. Between 1961 and 1963 he made a number of sculptures about the process of making or knowing, such as *Box with the Sound of Its Own Making* or *Three Rulers*. Of special relevance to the time and motion conveyed by the fists and fingers in these works of 1982 is an untitled lead piece of 1962. It appears to be a cut-away section revealing, in profile, a bulletlike missile and the track of its motion through the object. From this period also date small sculptures of body parts.

Process also concerned Morris in the sculptures labeled Minimal that he made from the early 1960s until 1967. In these he explored the fundamental nature of forms invented and imposed by humankind in the process of making things: "the basic infrastructure of forming itself." Subsequently, in the Anti-Form sculptures begun around 1967, the process of creation comes to the fore as part of the content. Unlike Minimal sculpture, these works display a nonauthoritarian process relying upon chance and indeterminacy.

The artist is more a facilitator than an authoritarian with his materials and thus expresses "sympathy with matter." In his works of the 1980s, Morris no longer is concerned with the process of creation but with its opposite, destruction.

The status of things in the world is one of Morris's longstanding interests; the chaos in this first series of reliefs presents a new viewpoint. The works from 1961 to 1963 focus on how we know about things; the Minimal sculptures are about things manufactured by humankind; Anti-Form art deals with things apart from authoritarian systems; and the works in this exhibition are about things in chaos and impending or actual destruction. But now the things are human rather than inanimate bodies. In the 1980s Morris is overtly raising questions of human destiny and addressing issues that are more immediately "personal" and less abstractly "philosophical." —*IMD*

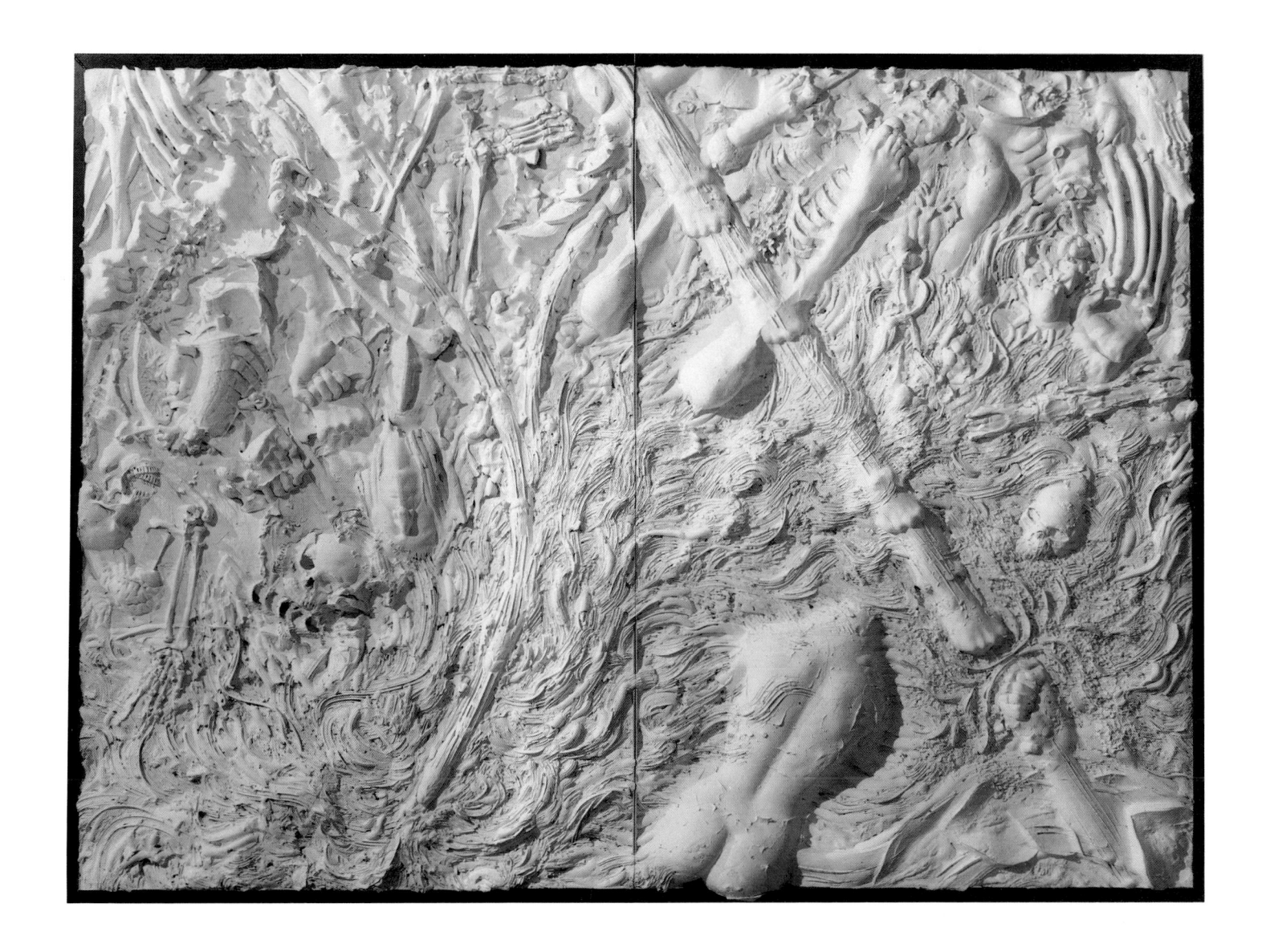

4 *Untitled*, 1955/83
painted cast Hydrocal, ink on
paper
33¼ x 51⅜ in. (84.5 x 130.5 cm)
Collection of the artist

The group of framed works made in 1983, in addition to no
longer being all white, are markedly different from the *Hypnerotomachia* series. Here Morris employs bilateral symmetry or
rhythmic, wavelike patterns; the impression of chaos is greatly
lessened. Two-dimensional drawings are incorporated within the
Hydrocal—a feature that in subsequent series of painted works
will reach the point where the Hydrocal frame becomes as
important as the contained work of art.

The incorporation of drawings from 1955 in each of these
pieces focuses our attention on time, since works from the past
are introduced into a context expressing anxiety for the future.
Cat. 4 incorporates drawings that have the look of Renaissance
or Baroque sketches, thus introducing another layer of time.
The drawing on the right of cat. 4 is of a nude male with arms
pulled sharply behind his back, a Michelangelesque bound
slave. Whether he is actually bound or not is uncertain, but it is
tempting to think so in light of the relief images which show
heavy rope interacting with feet, fists, a face, and phalluses.
This is an image of violence and bondage.

In the drawings in cat. 5, 6, and 7, figures executed in a
spiky, thornlike manner appear to be in motion (dancing?
fighting?). In the frame of cat. 5, a circle at the top resembles a
sun and the figures in the drawing coalesce into a configuration
that suggests a tree. The relief above the drawing continues the
tree form, branching out and mingling with arcs made by the
tracks of phalluses. It is as though rising out of the debris at the
bottom center are potent, seminal forces binding with organic
nature and the sun—almost denying chaos and affirming sympathy with matter and the universe. In the context of the anxiety
and doom pervading the work of the 1980s, this particular relief
is an exception, but even in this work there is a dark side.

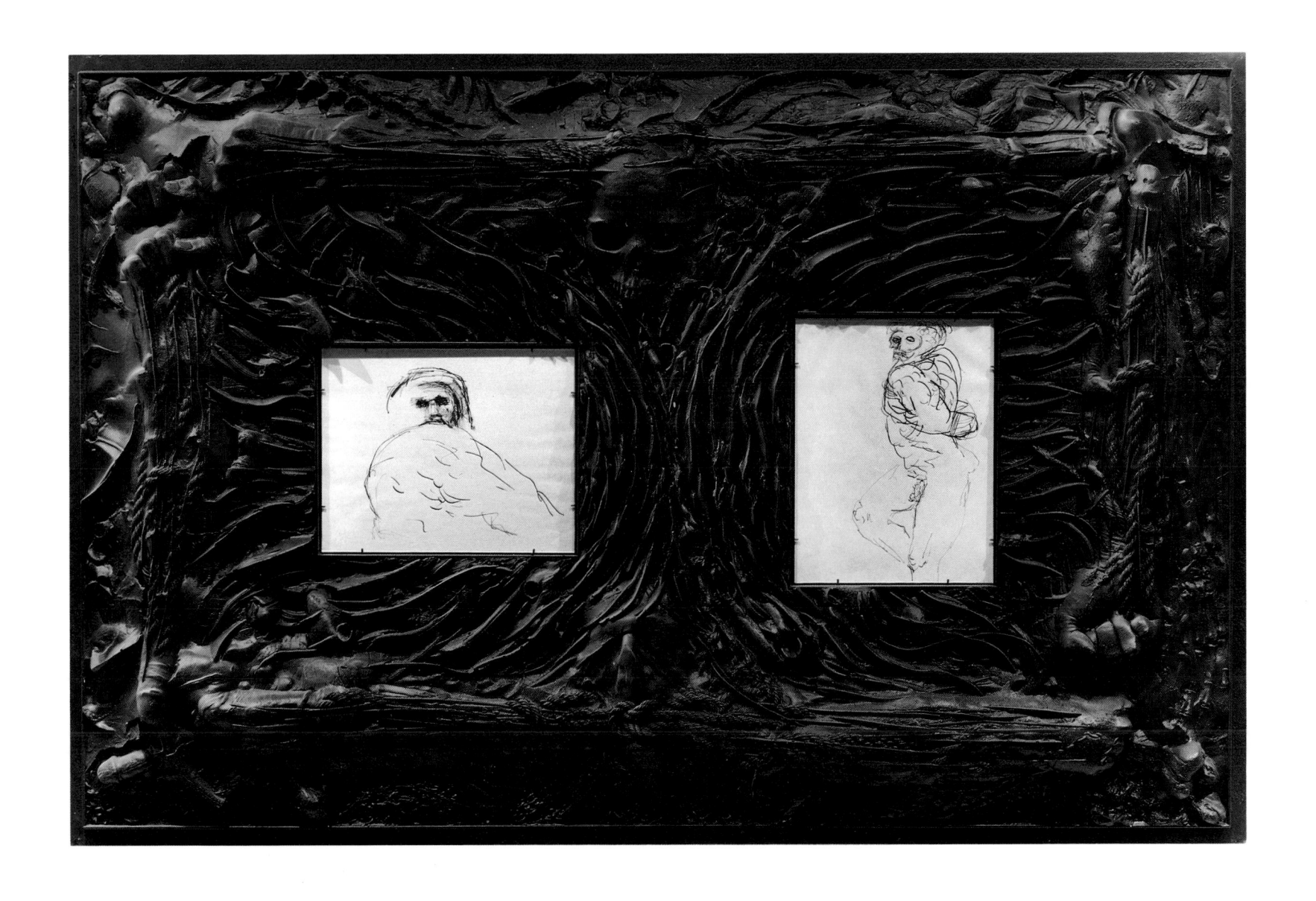

5   *Untitled*, 1955/83
painted cast Hydrocal, graphite
on paper
56 x 66 in. (142.2 x 167.6 cm)
Courtesy Sonnabend Gallery and
Leo Castelli Gallery, New York

Indeed, there is a dark side to all the decorative beauty one
sees in the design and increasing use of color in these reliefs.
Like Duchamp, Morris is more concerned with issues than
visual delectation. What does the surge of beauty in these works
have to do with doom or war? For Morris, the decorative can be
seen as "the ultimate response to a pervasive death anxiety";
sensuous beauty is not simply something in which to revel but a
statement of dissolution. —*IMD*

6   *Untitled*, 1955/83
    cast Hydrocal, graphite on paper
    55¾ x 65½ in. (141.6 x 166.4 cm)
    Courtesy Sonnabend Gallery and
    Leo Castelli Gallery, New York

7   *Untitled*, 1955/83
    cast Hydrocal, graphite on paper
    55¾ x 65½ in. (141.6 x 166.4 cm)
    Courtesy Sonnabend Gallery and
    Leo Castelli Gallery, New York

Robert Morris's interest in the perception of art through the senses, the process of making a work of art, and the idea of time has been evident in his work throughout his career. These interests come together in the invention of a process dependent on time and the deprivation of the senses (here, sight) and the elimination of eye and hand coordination to produce three series of drawings entitled *Blind Time*. These grew out of an interest in making drawings in a new way; up until then Morris's drawings were diagrams for sculpture. With *Blind Time* he wanted to make drawings that were related to earlier traditions but were new and specifically his own.

The first of these series (*Blind Time I*), dating from 1973, was executed by the artist who, having defined a particular drawing task (related to pressure, distance, location, geometric figures, and so on), estimated the length of time necessary to make the desired work, closed his eyes, and drew it on paper with his fingers, using graphite mixed with plate oil. Of the 98 examples in this series, many are divided in half symmetrically and usually the task is noted in pencil in the margin along with the difference between the time it took to make the work and the original estimation.

As a corollary project (*Blind Time II*), in 1976 Morris engaged to make drawings for him a woman who had been blind since birth (known to us only as "A.A."), whom he found through the American Association of the Blind. A procedure for making art that he had used for Minimal works (where an assistant or company was employed to carry out the actual fabrication), it seemed appropriate to create blind drawings by using such a "qualified" assistant. Directed by Morris, who specified the tasks, "A.A." made drawings by applying etching ink with her fingers. Sparer and less controlled than the artist's own blind drawings, they are more about her impressions and feelings; Morris added to them texts from their conversations. Ultimately, not esthetically satisfied with the results, Morris withdrew the 52 works that were the product of this collaboration.

8 *Blind Time III*, 1985
   graphite on paper
   38 x 50 in. (96.5 x 127 cm)
   Courtesy Sonnabend Gallery and
   Leo Castelli Gallery, New York

Inscription: *Working blindfolded for an estimated 6 minutes. The hands attempt to rub out vertical bands with progressively lighter pressure toward the edges of the page.*

In the experiments, single, unobserved photons passing through built the wave-like interference pattern. When observed they did not. In some sense the unwatched photons passed through both slits at once.

Time estimation error: +32 sec.

9 *Blind Time III*, 1985
   graphite on paper
   38 x 50 in. (96.5 x 127 cm)
   Courtesy Sonnabend Gallery and
   Leo Castelli Gallery, New York

Inscription: *Working blindfolded for an estimated 4 minutes the fingers attempt to rub out a grid on the left, then progress toward the right, distance being proportional to amount of hand contact with the pace and pressure inversely proportional to distance traveled. Later erasing is done.*

From models based on discreteness, causality, and harmony to those of indeterminacy, probabilities, violence, discontinuities and entropy. Feynman diagram of pair annihilation erased from memory.

Time estimation error: −11 sec.

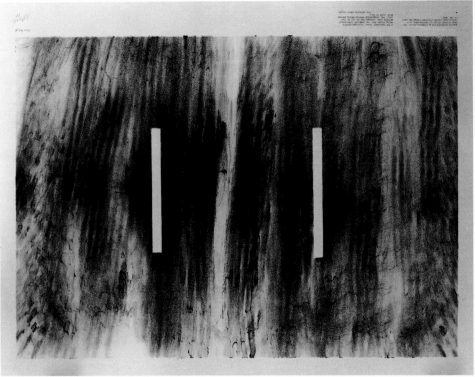

Blind Time III, 1985
graphite on paper
38 x 50 in. (96.5 x 127 cm)
Courtesy Sonnabend Gallery and
Leo Castelli Gallery, New York

Inscription: *Working blindfolded for
an estimated 7 minutes, a grid is
attempted in the lower left area.
Then the left hand applies twice the
amount of pressure as the right in an
estimated one-third area of the page,
the right hand follows the movement
of the left, expanding and elaborating
on its motion.*

*Searching for a metaphor for the
occupation of that moment between
lapsed time and possibilities spent on
the one hand, and an imagined but
unoccupiable future on the other, both
of which issue from that tightly woven
nexus of language, tradition and
culture which constructs our narrative
of time.*

Time estimation error: −35 sec.

Morris's most current series, *Blind Time III*, differs from those of over ten years ago. While still based on the same technical structure—Morris applies, by hand, graphite mixed with plate oil according to a prescribed task that he has set out to accomplish in a specified number of minutes, noting this procedure in the margin—he also brings into play through accompanying text the dictates and philosophy of physics, especially as it relates to perception and our notion of reality. Perception is a factor in both art and science. Our perception of the world is recorded and interpreted by artists. In the field of science, Albert Einstein at the beginning of this century proposed that reality is limited by our perception: we are aware only within the limits of our human senses and, moreover, space and time are forms of intuition that do not have an objective reality but exist only relative to our own perception, hence the laws of relativity.

In cat. 8, Morris created a rubbing with two parallel vertical bands left untouched. This composition suggests Morris's interpretation of the so-called double-slit experiment which is also referred to in the accompanying text. This experiment, by registering the path of photons, presents evidence for the particle character and wave nature of light. However, we are not able to observe both properties simultaneously. The acceptance of this is not contradictory but complementary, as stated in Niels Bohr's principle of complementarity, a keystone of quantum theory.

Morris refers in cat. 9 to the transition from a Newtonian world-view based on causality to an Einsteinian world of relativity based on statistics and the principle of uncertainty. The crisis created by this shift in thought was nowhere more pronounced than in the person of Einstein himself, who expressed the hope that the statistical method of quantum physics was not the final answer ("God does not play dice") and maintained a belief in a universe of order and harmony. To this thought Morris added a reference to the quantum electrodynamics of Richard Phillips

Feynman, who hypothesized about the interaction of electrons; his diagram for the annihilation of two particles is used graphically here by Morris who, through erasure, inscribed it into his smearings.

In cat. 10 Morris wrote about his search for a metaphor relating to our sense of time and a time continuum. Einstein's hypothesis states that our sense of time is a form of perception measurable only in relation to other events; the sequence of events creates a "narrative of time." Morris employs the grid, a man-made, measured graphic form, as a symbol for the reality we have built throughout history (i.e., "a tightly woven nexus of language, tradition, and culture").

Cat. 11 presents a diagram for the universe viewed as a "self-excited circuit" according to the physicist John Archibald Wheeler; on the left appears Morris's grid, symbolizing organized culture in which man can clearly place himself and function within the universe. Wheeler's diagram consists of the universe shown as the letter "U," which starts at the right with the big bang, the hypothesized beginning of the universe represented by Wheeler as a point but by Morris as a swirling smear, a spiral of cosmic soup. The universe grows in size from these beginnings, giving rise to life, containing observers (us) outfitted with observing equipment (symbolized by the great eye); this equipped observer Wheeler calls the "anthropic witness." Following along the basic quantum physics tenet of Bohr, that "no elementary phenomenon is a phenomenon until it is a recorded phenomenon," Wheeler hypothesized that no reality is a reality until it is observed. In both cases the observer plays an active role as a participant. Our particular understanding of the beginnings of the universe is influenced and guided by our perceptual capabilities, dictated by our observing equipment. Through observation we give tangible reality to the first moments of the universe (represented by the eye seeing the big bang). Morris extends this to the possibility that we can likewise give tangible reality to the last moments of existence. Feynman's diagram of proton decay makes further reference to this demise of matter.

In all of these *Blind Time* drawings, Morris's technique of smearing and rubbing surfaces creates nebulous shapes that point to both the unformed, chaotic state of things (as in the beginning of the universe) and the broken-apart dissolution of form (as would characterize the end). The look of these drawings, while achieved through a dictated, mechanical process, aptly describes a simultaneous state of becoming and dispersion that speaks to the philosophical interests of the artist and certain leading theoretical physicists. —*MJJ*

11 *Blind Time III*, 1985
graphite on paper
38 x 50 in. (96.5 x 127 cm)
Courtesy Sonnabend Gallery and
Leo Castelli Gallery, New York

Inscription: *Working blindfolded for an estimated 5 minutes a small grid is attempted on the left, then a spiral on the right which moves across to the grid. Then an eye is made which originates in the spiral but touches the grid. Then erasing is done.*

Grid as metaphor for the nexus of language, tradition and culture which gives rise to an ego-centric world view necessitating an anthropic witness who collapses the wave function and gives reality to even the first moments of the universe—and perhaps the last. Feynman diagram of proton decay erased from memory.

Time estimation error: —11"

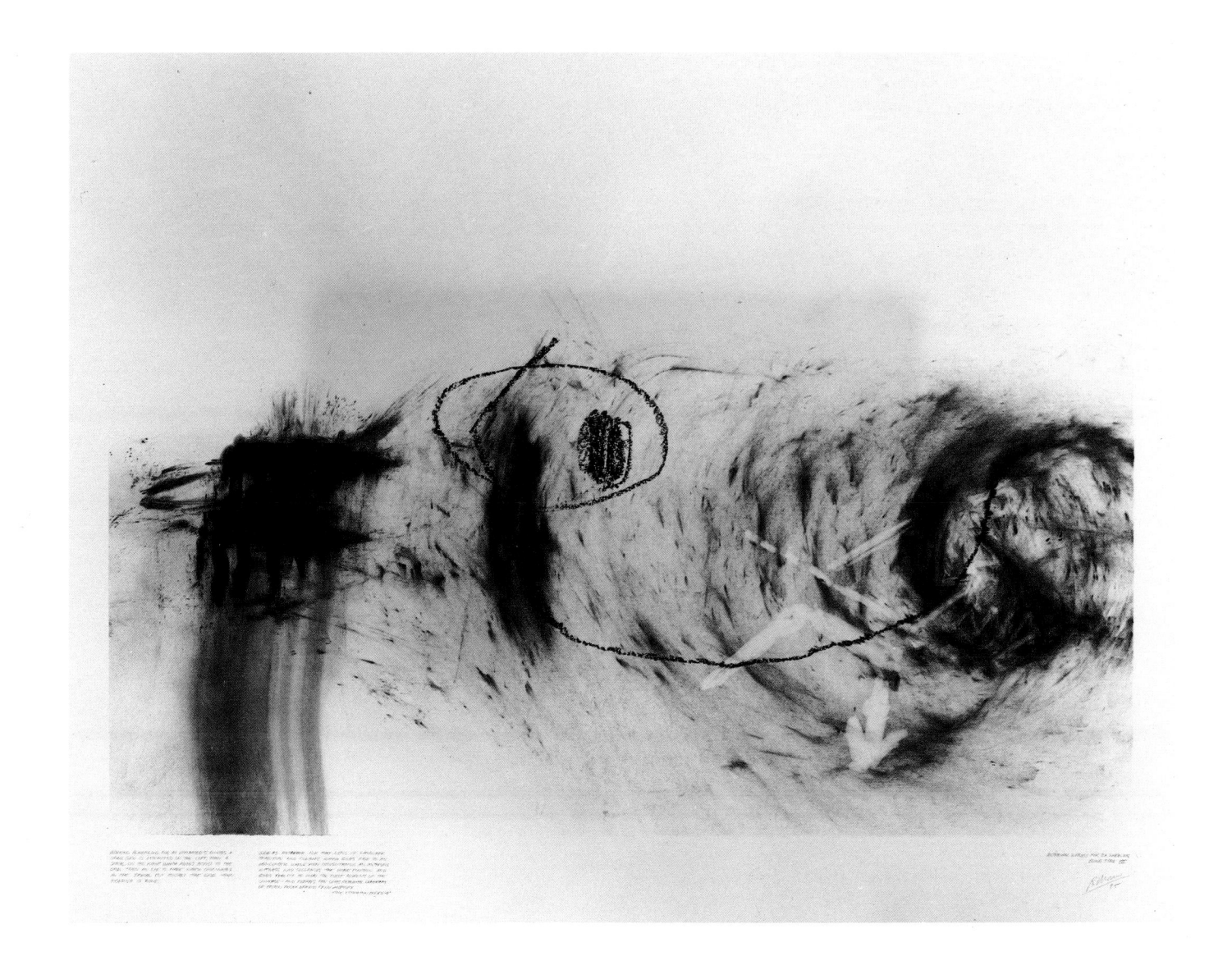

12   *Untitled (Firestorm series)*, 1982
ink, charcoal, graphite, and black
pigments on paper
6 panels, each 38 x 50 in.
(96.5 x 127 cm)
Overall: 76 x 150 in. (190.3 x 381 cm)
Courtesy Sonnabend Gallery and
Leo Castelli Gallery, New York

During 1983 Robert Morris completed two groups of large-scale multipanel drawings, the *Firestorm* and *Psychomachia* series. (*Psychomachia* refers to an early Latin poem by Prudentius in which the forces of good and evil battle for the spirit of man.) Morris's *Psychomachia* series represents a writhing, defeated humanity suspended in a nether world of abstraction and two-dimensional space, lost in a sea of explosive chaos. Similar to Morris's later series (the cast Hydrocal and pastel drawings), these works combine two scales, the broad overview and the intimate, albeit gruesome, detail.

In the *Psychomachia* and *Firestorm* series, the panoramic vision of a burning sky forms an environment in which lifesize figurative elements are intermeshed. Here the traditional figure/ground relationship is undermined. The drawings envelop the viewer in an atmosphere of smoldering fires, eruptive hot spots, and the ash and soot of cataclysm, creating a space where phantom figures intertwine rhythmically with human skeletons. Figurative elements are clustered, with large passages left open to reveal the burning atmosphere; only geometric elements, suggesting architecture, intersect the composition either vertically (cat. 12 and 13) or horizontally (cat. 14). The figures and architectural elements continue beyond the edge of the picture, revealing only a portion of the nightmarish wasteland.

Using combinations of media—ink, charcoal, graphite, and powdered pigments—Morris achieves a variety of techniques simultaneously; fine linear detail is combined with broad tonal harmonies. The surface is richly patterned in contrasts of light and dark, resulting in a baroque sculptural quality; an overall effect of emanating light is achieved. The drawings contain evidence of the artist's hand at work: the traces of his fingertips and palms are a constant reminder of the creative process. As he has done before, Morris explores the limits of a given material or technique. While the shapes are both dramatic and have form beyond pattern, the drawings remain essentially two-dimensional compositions with a very shallow space—no perspective, no point of focus, no beginning and no end. The resulting images resemble photographic negatives, the world

13   *Untitled (Psychomachia series),*
1982
ink, charcoal, graphite, and black
pigments on paper
14 panels, each 50 x 38 in.
(127 x 96.5 cm)
Overall: 100 x 266 in.
(254 x 675.6 cm)
Courtesy Sonnabend Gallery and
Leo Castelli Gallery, New York

reversed (solarized, as in a Man Ray photograph), and then
x-rayed (as in Rauschenberg), as though Ingres's *Turkish Bath*
had been hit by an incendiary device.

The Futurists, who reveled in the power and might of the
industrial war machine, caught the human figure in motion.
Morris, who is both attracted to and repelled by the capacity of
war in the twentieth century, presents his similarly interlocking
figures in relatively flat arrangements as though viewed from
above. Here, no Futurist motion is depicted but, instead, a
depersonalized heap of humanity burned beyond recognition.
These are not particular persons in a particular firestorm; the
features of one are indistinguishable from another. Although
these stenciled figures are mere shadows of human beings, an
enormous power struggle persists among them. Fists are
clenched tightly, hands and legs kick and flay, bodies twist and
contort in a last death struggle.

Many of the figures have a fleshy outerimage (achieved by re-
orienting the stencil) which gives the effect of an afterimage or
aura, yet the bodies themselves appear almost transparent, with
far greater emphasis given to skeletal structure. The skeletal
parts have an extraordinary verisimilitude to x-ray images of
human bodies, with such detail as to allow identification of
most of the major bones. The floating bones, which would not
remain in place in real skeletons, are accurately represented in
their proper anatomical positions in these x-ray-derived images.

It is important to note that the *Psychomachia* and *Firestorm*
drawings were executed immediately prior to the cast Hydrocal
and pastel works. In the more recent Hydrocal/pastel series
(cat. 16 through 22), the geometric shape of the frame functions
as an equivalent to both bars and labyrinth structures in the
Psychomachia and *Firestorm* drawings. Similarly, cast body
parts in the frames of the later works function as an equivalent
to the earlier figurative details; and the central atmospheric
portion of the Hydrocal/pastels has its counterpart in the explosive atmosphere of the *Psychomachia* and *Firestorm* works. In
all cases, the figure is presented in actual human scale. In the
Hydrocal/pastel works, overview and detail are separated in

14 *Untitled (Psychomachia series),*
    1982
    ink, charcoal, graphite, and black
    pigments on paper
    18 panels, each 38 x 50 in.
    (96.5 x 127 cm)
    Overall: 114 x 300 in.
    (289.6 x 762 cm)
    Courtesy Sonnabend Gallery and
    Leo Castelli Gallery, New York

the frame and pastel areas, respectively. In *Psychomachia* and *Firestorm*, however, atmospheric overview, human detail, and geometry are superimposed in unspecific planes that overlap. Combining discordant scales with the aforementioned uses of x-ray, reversal (negative), and solarization creates a complex, sandwiched vision.

While recognizing the iconography in these drawings, it is equally important to note that these works are untitled and nonspecific in nature. The compression of time, collaging of scale, and reordering of planar reality provides a formal context in which the struggle between good and evil for man's soul is investigated. Morris creates works of monumental stature which reveal as much about the process of drawing as the subject they explore.—*PS*

15 *On the Death of My Father,*
September 22, 1983, 1983
cast iron
22½ x 49½ in. (57.2 x 125.7 cm)
Collection of Mr. Asher B.
Edelman, New York

While this work commemorates the death of the artist's father, it occurred at a point in Morris's career when he was steeped in the use of *memento mori*, traditional reminders of the inevitability of death and moral symbols of human vanity. Using cast sculptural elements that had made their appearance the previous year as body parts imbedded in a devastating disorder in his *Hypnerotomachia* series of reliefs, here he formalized these elements into symmetrical, yet vigorously energized, compositions. The arrangement takes on a decorativeness as the sinuous, flowing forms recall the art nouveau style; the hands at the bottom, for instance, become a framing device as they curve around and upward.

In a great swirl of force, a battery of clenched fists physically rips apart the picture, pulling open an image that once was whole. Below, below the heavens that have been parted, below the ground of the earth, spreading out left and right, are fetuses that become human skulls—symbols of birth to death—a continuum broken by the separation at the center. And finally, in the bottom third, two hands with open palms and long tentacled fingers that become phalluses—symbols of male aggression and power—sweep the picture apart. Clearly indicated is the trajectory traveled by the fists, skulls, and hands. This is a physical art marked by the artist's fingers, just as he made his *Blind Time* series, without the aid of a tool. Unlike the more static *Hypnerotomachia*, or his lead works of the 1960s such as *Hand and Toe Holds* of 1964, we see implied movement. Even moreso than his 1962 study of a bullet's trajectory (fig. 4), where time and impact are frozen, here we sense the ongoing motion of unrelenting cosmic time.

The preexisting integrity of the image as a whole is evident. But the force of separation is great—separation from life to death, a father from son, of existence to nonexistence. It is a rupture that will not be restored. The deathlike finality is emphasized by Morris's use of black cast iron instead of the white, soft Hydrocal of *Hypnerotomachia*. This work coincides with Morris's use of plaster frames in which he placed some of his 1955 drawings. The cast elements in these frames range from swirling images in disparate order with occasional skulls or hands visible, to more symmetrical arrangements whose power is heightened by interlocked rigid elements as characterized in *On the Death of My Father*. Moreover, this pivotal, personal work foreshadows Morris's use of sculptural elements in his painted works beginning in the same year in which his father died. —*MJJ*

Figure 4
Bullet Trajectory, c. 1963
lead
Collection of Dr. and Mrs.
Marvin H. Grody

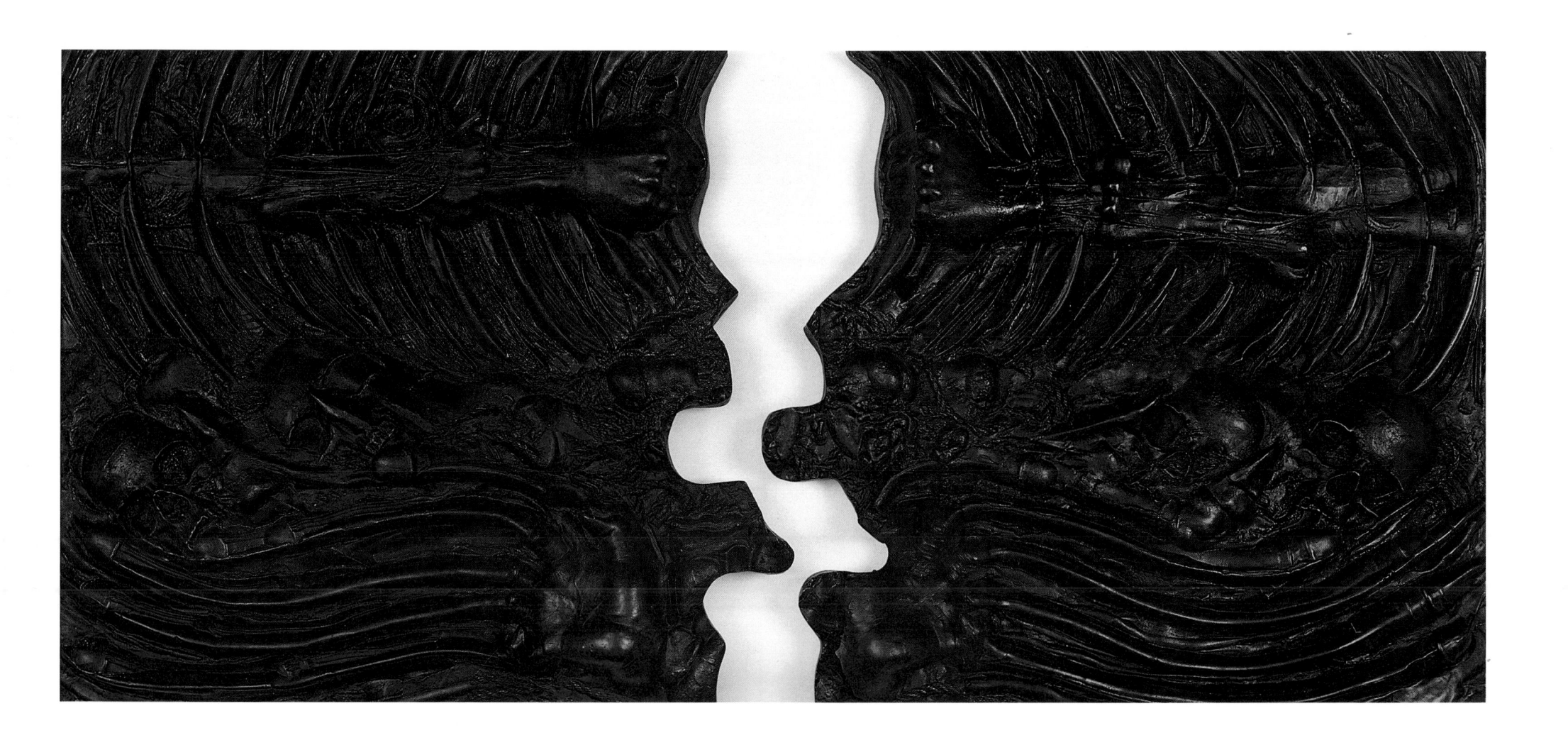

16   *Untitled*, 1983
         painted cast Hydrocal, pastel on
         paper
         84 x 100 in. (213.4 x 254 cm)
         Collection of Robert and Nancy
         Kaye, New York

Bringing together the smeared, swirling look and use of accompanying text of his *Blind Time* and *Firestorm* drawings with the sculptural devices of his *Hypnerotomachia* reliefs, Morris in 1983 began creating a stirring body of framed, painted works. As in *On the Death of My Father*, the main sculptural motifs are skulls, arms with clenched fists, and hands with open palms and fingers streaming outward to become, usually, phalluses. Symbols of power, male aggression, warfare, combined with death, they are organized symmetrically and take on the quality of a decorative motif, even to the point (in cat. 22) of forming an egg-and-dart cornice design of vaginas and penises; sexuality and power become one. In this same work Morris attached separate, additional sculptural elements at the right and bottom whose forms are echoed at the left by a skeletal hand enmeshed in concentric curves of vinelike substances; from three sides they all push towards the bright light at the painting's center. (In his subsequent *Burning Planet* series, sculptural appendages become even more pronounced, the frames open up, and metal constructs extend the scene.)

The velocity and movement of these traditional *memento mori* both reflect the terror felt in contemplating the possible destruction of the universe by nuclear holocaust and allude to eventual natural apocalypse. They also, however, give visual form to the breakdown of matter that lies at the base of such occurrences, whether man-induced or not. The opposing paths of the body parts which Morris depicts and the "tails" they create by their implied velocity find relationship to the action of atoms, whose speed and reaction upon being split send particles off into opposing directions. Morris's body elements undergo within these frames a process of nuclear fission in a self-sustaining chain reaction. In physics, the disintegration of the atom breaks the nucleus into two main fragments, emitting neutrons that cause fission of additional atoms. In Morris's work, body parts (fist against fist, hand against hand) are divided into two, paralleling this nuclear reaction. The multiplication of forms (fist upon fist upon fist) further articulates a chain reaction.

17 *Untitled*, 1983-84
painted cast Hydrocal, watercolor
and pastel on paper
102 x 108 x 21 in.
(259 x 274.3 x 53.3 cm)
The Rivendell Collection,
New York

In fission, matter is converted into energy, a principle that underlies the atomic bomb, whose detonation first proved that man could convert matter into light, heat, sound, motion— that is, forms of energy. This implosion bomb mounted against the nuclei caused an act of chemical violence, creating pressure so great that fission occurred. In Morris's paintings the human body undergoes a pressure that forces it to transcend its form. As body parts disperse into force lines and move with the velocity of atoms, Morris gives visual evidence to Einstein's theory of the conversion of matter into energy. The frames do not depict severed bodies that are remnants of an explosion, but the substance from which an implosion takes place. Imploding inward to the nucleus of the painting, human life is converted to light and heat, with sensations of sound and motion; pure energy is formed. While this is the action of nuclear physics as produced by man and accelerated by means of warfare, it also foretells the inevitable entropy of the universe toward which all phenomena of nature are moving. Nature moves in one direction, toward a state of greater randomness, entropy. The universe is perhaps progressing toward an ultimate "heat-death," a condition of maximum entropy, according to the Second Law of Thermodynamics. It is this heat-death, the imploding universe and impending doom, that Morris shows us. These paintings tell of this inherent inevitability, not solely the outcome of nuclear warfare.

The *memento*, the warning, inherent in these works is an admonition to science. The vanity of man in the face of God has been replaced by the knowledge of the scientist in the face of eternity. History has told us that the technological imperative propels humanity to use such means: the world was on the brink of an end to the war, Germany having surrendered and Japan seeking peace negotiations when, on August 6 and 9, 1945, the first atomic bombs were dropped on Hiroshima and Nagasaki. Once the bomb existed, putting it to use seemed inevitable. Today, President Reagan's Strategic Defense Initiative ("Star Wars") carries with it the same credibility and possibility. Even

18 *Untitled*, 1984
    painted cast Hydrocal, oil on
    canvas
    69½ x 86½ in. (176.5 x 219.7 cm)
    Collection of Gerald S. Elliott,
    Chicago

*Inscription: Firestorm winds of
hurricane force collapsed walls and
sucked away the oxygen. Its heat
melted metal roofs and blew showers
of molten sparks which burnt holes in
the corneas of their eyes.*

in today's non-wartime period, American scientists drift from humanistic purposes to destructive, military ones. (An earlier key example is physicist Ernest Lawrence, whose contribution in nuclear physics and atomic energy linked with that of J. Robert Oppenheimer made the atomic bomb possible, but whose initial role was in the application of nuclear physics for medical research, particularly cancer.) Of this Morris is well aware. This technological imperative has the capacity to bring about a man-made apocalypse. Is there a death wish for oneness in which mind and body are united as all become pure energy? Oppenheimer foresaw this sense of oneness as matter became energy, calling the first detonation of the atomic bomb "Trinity."

Here one understands the dual emotions associated with the apocalypse. This Morris noted in 1981 in his *Restless Sleepers/Atomic Shrouds* (fig. 5), for which he incorporated a text in the design of this bedsheet. He expanded this quotation the following year in a drawing in which he coupled a text from the physicist Ted Taylor and Leonardo's notebook. In describing the effects of an imploding bomb, Taylor stated that it creates conditions that "are quite different perhaps from anything else that happens in the universe, unless there are other people who make bombs." Leonardo had already served as a source for Morris, who had appropriated his *Deluge* drawings for use in his photo-history of the making of the bomb in *Jornada del Muerto, (from "The Natural History of Los Alamos")* of 1981. In this quotation the Renaissance artist/scientist stated his fascination upon encountering a huge cavern whose mystery awakened in him two emotions—fear and desire: "fear of the dark threatening cavern, desire to see whether there might be any marvelous thing therein." One recalls here, as well, the exaltation and despair of the physicist Oppenheimer at the impressive sight of the detonation of the first atomic bomb. In this supreme scientific wonder of ultimate importance, sensations of the magnificent and seductive met head on with the horrific and repellent.

While the decorative style of Morris's painted works reflects, as he calls it, a "numbness," a decadence and loss of values and concern for our own mortality in the face of global threats, it is also a fitting mode to depict a scene at once seductive and horrifying. The world that man has created today through science allows us to imagine the unimaginable. In this way we can see the extreme of entropy, apocalypse, and make known to ourselves what the beginning of the universe must have been like as we view the end. Advanced scientific knowledge will, perhaps, as Oppenheimer predicted, come to a malignant conclusion as we follow the belief "that total knowlege is possible, that all that is potential can exist as actual." When man reaches the potential for producing total energy—or the perfect bomb—knowing what could be, he may feel compelled to make it happen. —*MJJ*

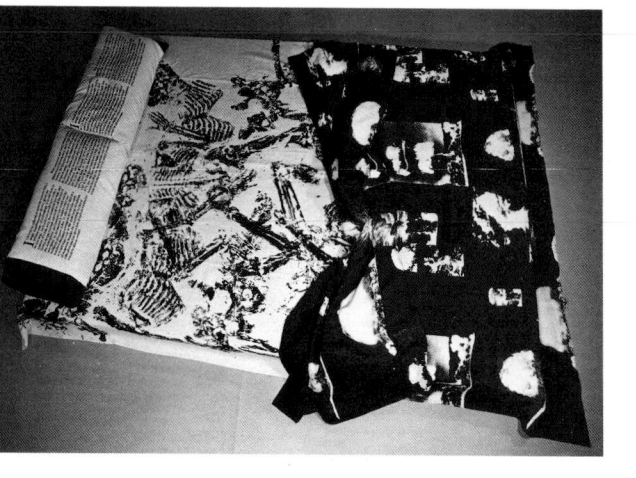

Figure 5
*Restless Sleepers/Atomic
Shrouds*, 1981
silkscreen on linen
Limited edition
sheets/pillowcases
produced by Fabric Workshop,
Philadelphia

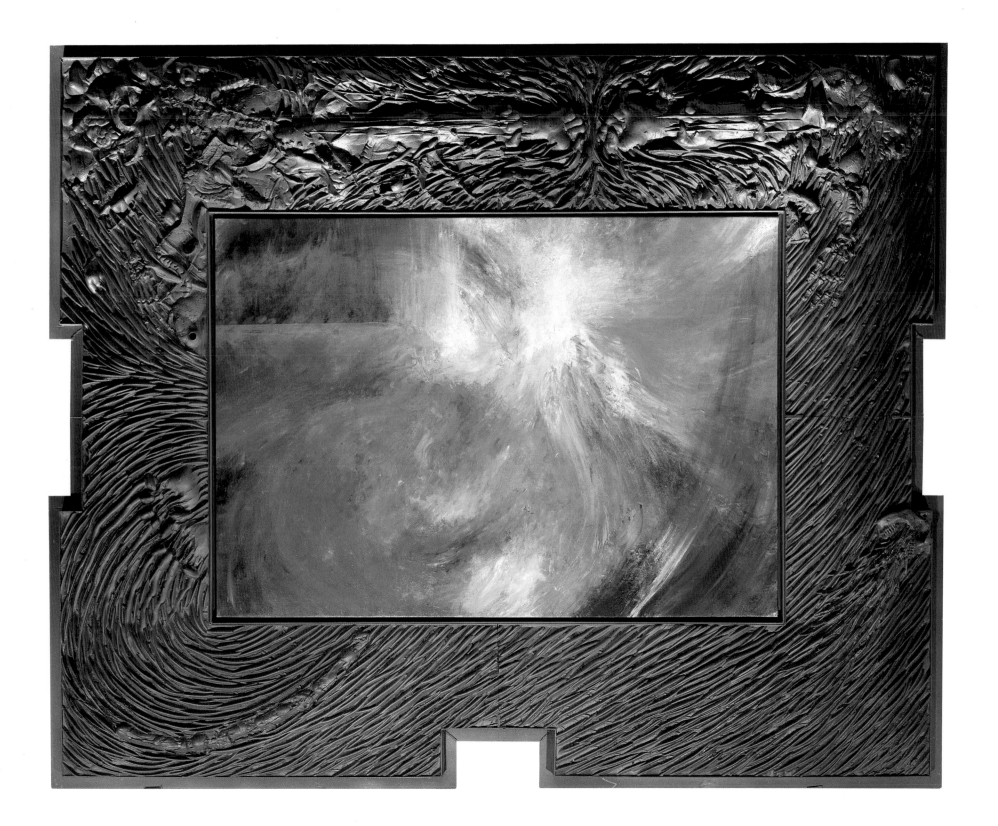

19 *Untitled*, 1984
    painted cast Hydrocal, pastel
    on paper
    65½ x 84¾ x 8 in.
    (166.4 x 215.3 x 20.3 cm)
    Collection of Sherry Fabrikant,
    New York

Inscription: *Concussion waves
(which leave no marks on the body),
incineration, fragmentation devices,
asphyxiation, flying glass, and melting
roofs that created a rain of molten lead
and copper on those below.*

In 1981–82 Morris created a series of cast Hydrocal relief works called *Hypnerotomachia* which were followed in 1983 by the monumental multipart drawings known as *Firestorm* and *Psychomachia*. As an artist recognized for his interest in combining disparate visual and material elements, it is logical that Morris would then combine the old and new by framing his 1955 drawings with reliefs (1983). From 1983 to 1984, Morris completed more than a dozen works incorporating brilliantly colored pastel-on-paper drawings in cast Hydrocal frames. These large-scale works were the first to resolve a main avenue of the artist's ongoing investigations: the combination of a variety of visual elements with a diversity of scales allowing the viewer to see simultaneously the big picture, the tight shot, and the narrative surrounding the piece.

The sculptural frame and pastel drawing elements in this series are visually and structurally interactive and interdependent. Morris begins with the drawing and then arranges objects for the cast frame. His frame both responds to and elaborates on the pastel drawing's compositional elements (e.g., horizon line). Creating a sculptural frame around the pastel resolves the problems of layering various elements of disparate scale (which occurred in *Psychomachia*) by separating figurative detail from atmospheric overview. As a fortunate outcome of this simplification, the work becomes far more complex and rich in specific iconographic detail.

These works are far less propagandistic, less rhetorical than earlier war- or death-related pieces by Morris (e.g., *Jornada del Muerto*, from "The Natural History of Los Alamos"). Only the intricate figurative details and the grandeur and sublime beauty of explosive landscapes are represented; no middle ground (context) is revealed—just art. By omitting visual reference to specific incidents, Morris creates powerful universal symbols, rather than logos or caricatures. While the works speak eloquently on the concerns of this time, their meaning is timeless. These are not simply antinuclear, anti-MX missile works. They delve more deeply into the undercurrents of man, exploring not the golden thread of life uncompromised, but the dark vein of evil, destruction, and annihilation.

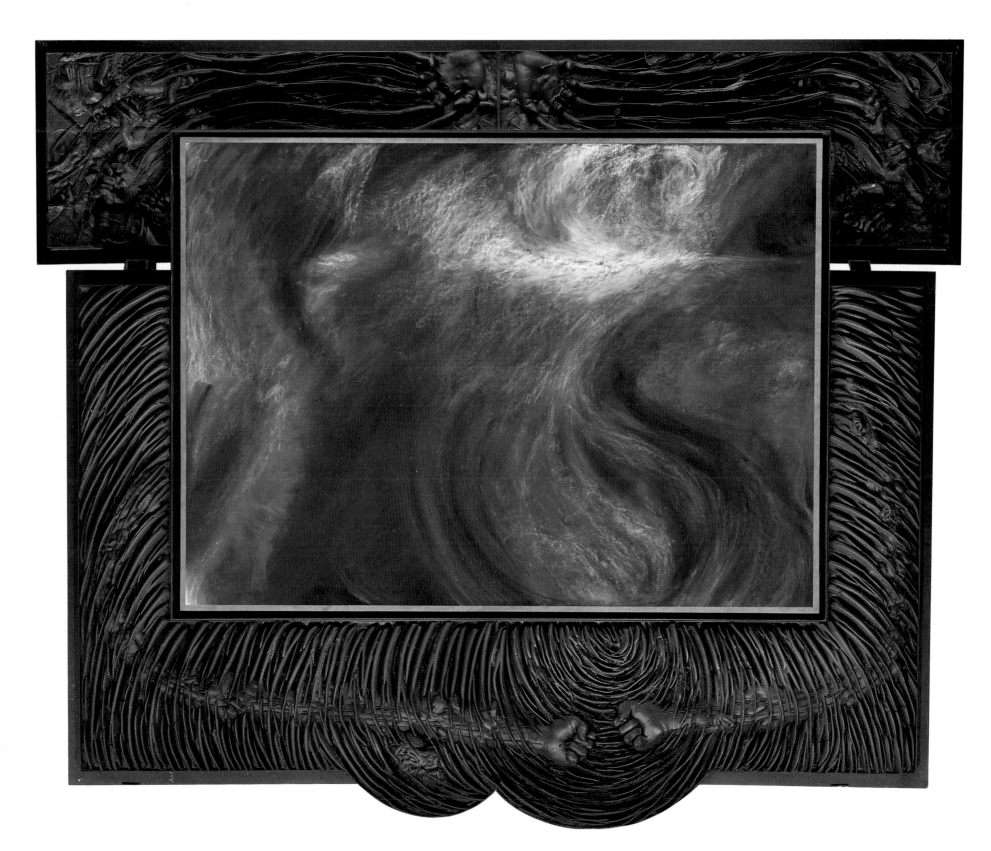

20 *Untitled*, 1984
painted cast Hydrocal, pastel
on paper
72 x 51 ¼ in. (182.9 x 130.2 cm)
Collection of Estelle Schwartz,
New York, courtesy Sonnabend
Gallery, New York

The Hydrocal/pastel works can be subdivided into three separate groups. In the first group are relatively simple rectangular compositions with continuous, uninterrupted frames. In these, the relationship between frame and drawing is not specific. The frame appears as a separate, sculptural element that merely encloses the pastel drawing. In the second grouping (cat. 19 and 21) the interplay is simple and clear: the drawings are divided horizontally in either the lower or upper third of the composition, and the frames are notched correspondingly, emphasizing the artificial horizon line—which does not separate earth from sky but instead divides the swirling atmosphere of the flames. In the third group (cat. 17 and 22) the interrelationship becomes far more complex: the bright red and yellow spot at the middle left edge of the pastel in cat. 22 has its counterpart in the form of a fist, with wakelike trailing lines, thrusting toward the drawing from the frame, as though its impact has created an explosion in the pastel. In the pastel of cat. 17, which represents elements of landscape and architecture, even more direct counterparts are evident in the linear patterns and figurative elements in the frame.

Morris further emphasizes the interdependency between the frame and drawing by painting the Hydrocal. This creates the illusion that objects in the frame are illuminated by the burning fires represented in the drawing. In cat. 17 and 18 not only are the frames lit by the glow of the pastel, but colors from the pastel appear to spill over onto the frame.

This new format encouraged the artist to work with watercolor, a material that had interested him for some time. By overlaying washes of watercolor, Morris has created a dark, nocturnal ground from which pastel explosions of light and color emanate. His shift from black, gray and white to extremely charged, dramatic colors coincides with his shift to a combination of pastel drawings and three-dimensional casting. The techniques Morris uses in applying the pastel are an extension of those he used with charcoal and black pigments in the monumental drawings of 1982. In combining watercolor with pastel and by painting the Hydrocal (which had previously been left in

21 *Untitled*, 1984
    painted cast Hydrocal, pastel
    on paper
    63½ x 73½ x 15 in.
    (161.3 x 186.7 x 38.1 cm)
    Private Collection, New York,
    courtesy Sonnabend Gallery,
    New York

Inscription: *None will be ready when it
touches down. Yet we have seen it
gathering all these years. You said
there was nothing that could be done.*

its natural color), Morris explores more subtly the relationship
between sculpture and drawing.

Through a process that involves both casting and direct carv-
ing, Morris builds an overwhelming array of detail in his frames.
He casts found and/or manufactured objects in plaster, subsequently carves directly into the plaster, and then recasts in
Hydrocal, allowing for both direct manipulation and accurate
verisimilitude of the original object. Key images and symbols
represented in the frames appear with great consistency throughout the series: skulls, fetuses, fists, genitals, and internal organs
(heart, brain) appear in many of the works. Although the frames
represent the devastation to humans in the aftermath of a firestorm or nuclear explosion, their overall composition is anything
but a disorderly heap of human refuse. The variety of objects
cast in Hydrocal are unified through the use of tendril-like lines
of force, swirling three-dimensionally, which emphasize the
flames of the pastel and create an integrated composition. In
some works, the text imbedded in the frame identifies specific
historical events. However, without this clue, there is no middle
ground to establish the place, time, and circumstance of the
depicted holocaust.

Regardless of the political or social iconography in these
works, there are several art historical precedents that inform
Morris's image. The pastels, in particular, may be considered
within the tradition of the abstract sublime landscape rather
than as representations of a holocaust. The central image can be
interpreted as a depiction of natural phenomena. As painters
who used nature and natural phenomena as symbols of the
human soul, nineteenth-century American Luminists such as
Thomas Cole, Frederic E. Church, and Albert Pinkham Ryder
provide one key to understanding these works. The pastel drawing in cat. 19 has qualities similar to nineteenth-century romantic
symbolist paintings of the Northern Lights, aurora borealis. The
Turneresque quality of cat. 16 is striking, and cat. 17 brings to
mind Whistler Nocturnes. Moreover, a precedent for evoking a
dense, steaming, swirling atmosphere can be found in Morris's
own work: in the mid-1970s, on the campus of the University of

22 *Untitled*, 1984
    painted cast Hydrocal, pastel
    on paper
    90½ x 95 x 11 in.
    (229.9 x 241.3 x 27.9 cm)
    Collection of Suzanne and Howard
    Feldman, New York

Inscription: *In Dresden, it was said afterwards that temperatures in the Allstadt reached 3000 degrees. They spoke of 250,000 dead. Wild animals from the destroyed zoo were seen walking among those leaving the ruined city.*

Washington in Bellingham, he created a work inspired by steam escaping from the subways in New York. By arranging an elaborate system of plumbing with reduction devices and perforated copper pipe, Morris caused steam to percolate up through a bed of river stones. The resulting atmosphere of vapor, which changed with the slightest breeze, has much in common visually with the atmosphere represented in these pastels.

These examples are important insomuch as they illustrate sources for Morris within the history of art, sources that have nothing to do with representations of war. Morris's works depict nature confronted by human invention.—*PS*

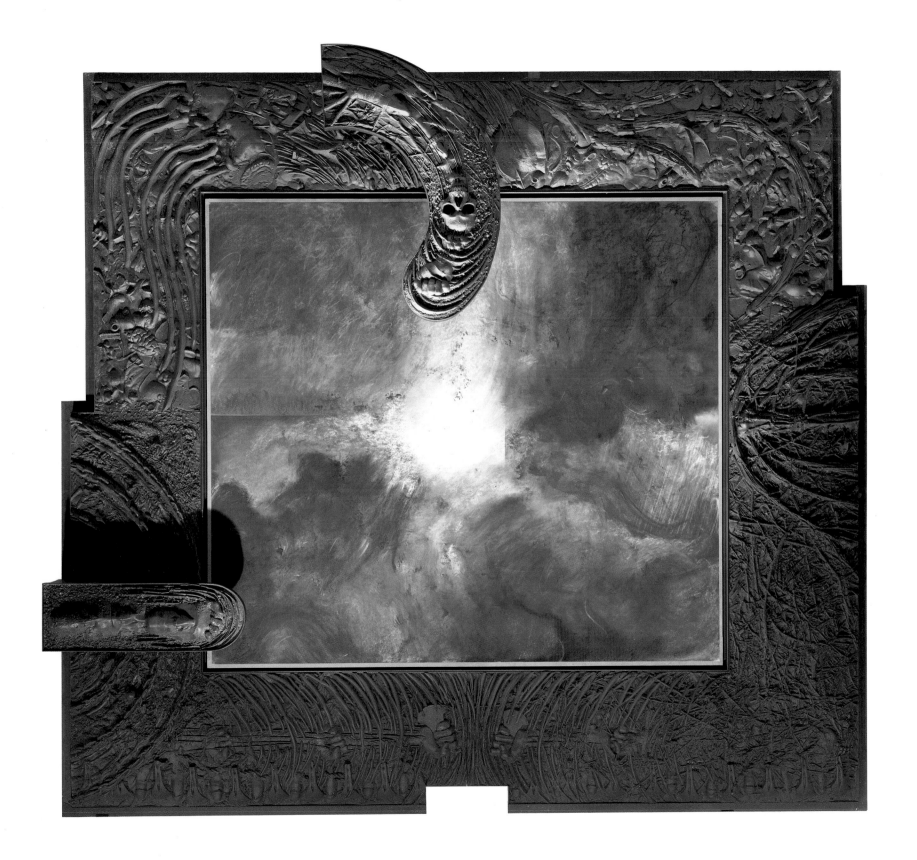

23   *The Anthropic Witness*, 1985
chalk, granite, and varnish on cast
fiberglass
264 x 72 in. (670.6 x 182.9 cm)
Courtesy Sonnabend Gallery
and Leo Castelli Gallery, New York

In this massive, tripartite construction, *The Anthropic Witness*, a concept described by physicist John Archibald Wheeler (see *Blind Time*), observes the cataclysmic moment of the universe. While Wheeler suggests that the witness, through observation, gives tangible reality to the earliest days of the universe (and these, according to the big bang theory, were indeed chaotic and violent), one is moved here to see this work instead as a depiction of the end rather than the beginning. Morris extended Wheeler's theory to place the witness, us, in the position of observing the last days of our universe. Here he shows us this moment.

In the form of a great cloud of doom, this ominous black shape hangs menacingly above our heads. Like the heavens parting, the seemingly once-contiguous halves separate to reveal a hellish scene of bodies and bones. Scattered body elements also appear in the surrounding sections and, throughout, the clenched fist maintains the dominant position it has assumed in much of Morris's art of this period. The naturalistic geological allusion to the rupture of the earth and the physical connection between the two halves is heightened by the texture and outline of these shapes, which were literally formed by making a cast in fiberglass of a boulder. The positive and negative halves of this mold are used here—two parts of the same element divided.

Inscribed in chalk, a major motif is Wheeler's anthropic witness: the big bang giving rise to the universe (the U-shape in fig. 6) which contains the observer who, in a self-reflexive mode, witnesses the big bang or, here, the apocalypse (the dotted line and arrow connect us to the beginning/end). Across the pit of death, an extension of the observer's vision is marked by the path of a white streak that leads to a spiral, a more graphic and vigorous depiction of the chaos of the universe as earlier added to Wheeler's diagram by Morris in cat. 11. The apocalypse we observe here points not only to our ability theoretically to know the end, thereby giving reality to it, but also to bring about the end—Wheeler's observer-participant taken to the extreme—as we employ our knowledge, propelled by the technological imperative, to "create" the end. The observer defines reality but can also *make* this holocaust, as Morris says, "giving reality to the last moments of the universe."—*MJJ*

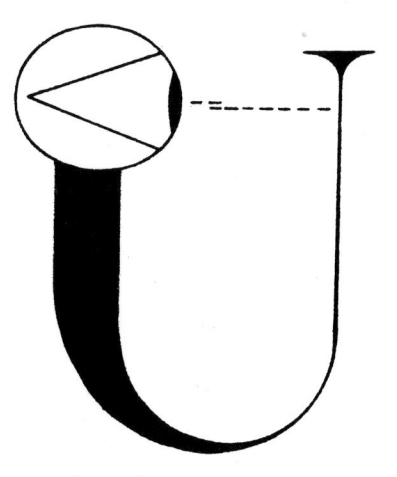

Figure 6
John Archibald Wheeler's
diagram of the Universe
viewed as a "self-excited
circuit"

Robert Morris

Born 1931, Kansas City, Missouri
Studied University of Kansas and Kansas City
   Art Institute, 1948–50; California School
   of Fine Arts, San Francisco, 1951; Reed
   College, Portland, Oregon, 1953–55;
   Hunter College, New York, 1961–62.

SELECTED EXHIBITION HISTORY
Selected one-person exhibitions of Morris's
work are listed in sections, with institutions
given for the period 1957-77 and titles of exhibitions and institutions given for the period 1978-85. Selected group exhibitions are given only for the period 1978-85.

Selected One-Person Exhibitions 1957–77
1957   Dilexi Gallery, San Francisco (also 1958)
1963   Green Gallery, New York (also 1964, 1965)
1967   Leo Castelli Gallery, New York (also 1968, 1969, 1972, 1976)
1968   Stedelijk van Abbemuseum, Eindhoven, Holland
       Galerie Ileana Sonnabend, Paris (also 1971, 1973, 1977)
1969   Galleria Enzo Sperone, Turin
       Irving Blum Gallery, Los Angeles (also 1970)
       The Corcoran Gallery of Art, Washington, D.C.
1970   The Detroit Institute of Arts
       Whitney Museum of American Art, New York
1971   The Tate Gallery, London
1973   Konrad Fischer Gallery, Düsseldorf
       Max Protetch Gallery, Washington, D.C.
       Galleriaforma, Genoa
       Lucio Amelio Modern Art Agency, Naples

Ace Gallery, Vancouver, Canada
       Ace Gallery, Venice, California
1974   Institute of Contemporary Art, University of Pennsylvania, Philadelphia
       Sonnabend Gallery and Leo Castelli Gallery, New York
       Galerie Art in Progress, Munich
       Alessandra Castelli Gallery, Milan
       Grand Rapids Project, Belknap Park, Grand Rapids, Michigan (Permanent Earthwork)
1975   D'Alessandro-Ferranti, Rome
1976   Leo Castelli Gallery and Sonnabend Gallery, New York
1977   The Louisiana Museum, Humlebaek, Denmark
       Williams College Museum of Art, Williamstown, Massachusetts
       James Corcoran Gallery, Los Angeles
       Portland Center for the Visual Arts, Oregon
       Stedelijk Museum, Amsterdam
       Reconstruction and Permanent Installation of "Observatory," Oostelijk Flevoland, Holland
       Galerie Art In Progress, Düsseldorf

Selected One-Person Exhibitions 1978–85
1978   "Blind Time II Drawings," Florence Wilcox Art Gallery, Swarthmore College, Swarthmore, Pennsylvania
1979   "Six Mirrors Works," Leo Castelli Gallery, New York
       "In the Realm of the Carceral," Sonnabend Gallery, New York
1980   "Robert Morris: Major Sculpture, Drawings and New Felt Pieces," Richard Hines Gallery, Seattle
       "Robert Morris: First Study for View From a Corner of Orion (Night) and Second Study for View From a Corner

of Orion (Day)," Leo Castelli/142 Greene Street, New York
       "Robert Morris," The Art Institute of Chicago
1981   "Robert Morris: Selected Works 1970–1981," Contemporary Arts Museum, Houston
1982   "The Drawings of Robert Morris," Sterling and Francine Clark Art Institute, organized by Williams College Museum of Art, Williamstown, Massachusetts (traveled in U.S. and Europe)
1983   "Psychomachia Drawings," Leo Castelli Gallery, New York
       "Hypnerotomachia Reliefs and Firestorm Drawings," Sonnabend Gallery, New York
       Krannert Art Museum, University of Illinois, Champaign
       Galerie Daniel Templon, Paris
       "Robert Morris: Tekeningen 1956–1983," Rijksmuseum, Amsterdam
1984   "Robert Morris: Recent Felt Pieces," Galerie Nordenhake, Malmö, Sweden
       "Robert Morris Installation," Malmö Kunsthall, Sweden
       Padiglione d'Arte Contemporanea di Milano, Italy
       Portland Center for Visual Art, Oregon
1985   "Robert Morris: Works from 1967–1984," Sonnabend Gallery, New York
       "Robert Morris: Works from 1967–1984," Leo Castelli Gallery/142 Greene Street, New York

Selected Group Exhibitions 1978–85
1978   "Hermetic Aspects of Contemporary Art," P.S. 1, Long Island City, New York, organized by Institute for Art & Urban Resources
       "Drawings for Outdoor Sculpture 1946–1977," Amherst College, Massachusetts, organized by John Weber Gallery, New York (traveled)
       "Salute to Merce Cunningham, John Cage and Collaborators," Thomas Segal Gallery, Boston
       "Structures for Behaviour," Art Gallery of Ontario, Toronto
       "Sculpture/Nature," Centre d'Arts Plastiques Contemporains de Bordeaux, France
       "Art About Art," Whitney Museum of American Art, New York (traveled)
       "Modern American Painting & Sculpture from the Dallas Museum of Fine Arts," Fort Worth Art Museum, Texas
       "About the Strange Nature of Money," Städtische Kunsthalle, Düsseldorf (traveled)
1979   "Supershow," Hudson River Museum, Yonkers, New York, organized by Independent Curators, Inc.
1980   "Leo Castelli: A New Space," Leo Castelli Gallery/142 Greene Street, New York
       "Three Installations: Acconci, Morris, Oppenheim," Sonnabend Gallery, New York
       "Hidden Desires," Neuberger Museum, State University of New York, Purchase
       "American Sculpture: Gifts of Howard & Jean Lipman," Whitney Museum of American Art, New York
       "Drawings: The Pluralist Decade,"

Institute of Contemporary Art, University of Pennsylvania, Philadelphia
"Venice Biennale 1980," U.S. Pavilion, Venice (traveled)
"Contemporary Sculpture, Selections from the Collection of the Museum of Modern Art," Museum of Modern Art, New York
"From Reinhardt to Christo," Allen Memorial Art Museum, Oberlin College, Ohio
"Exposition Société des Artistes Indépendents," Grand Palais, Paris
"The Minimal Tradition," The Aldrich Museum of Contemporary Art, Ridgefield, Connecticut
"Group Show," Sonnabend Gallery, New York
"Drawings/Structures," Institute of Contemporary Art, Boston
"Architectural Sculpture," Los Angeles Institute of Contemporary Art
"American Drawing in Black and White," The Brooklyn Museum, New York

1981 "Painting and Sculpture by Candidates for Art Awards," American Academy and Institute of Arts and Letters, New York
"Selections from Castelli: Drawings and Works on Paper," Neil G. Ovsey Gallery, Los Angeles
"International Ausstellung Köln 1981," Cologne
"Metaphor: New Projects by Contemporary Sculptors," Hirshhorn Museum and Sculpture Garden, Smithsonian Institution, Washington, D.C.

1982 "Antiform et Arte Povera, Sculptures 1966–69," Centre d'Arts Plastiques Contemporains de Bordeaux, France

The High Museum of Art, Atlanta, Georgia
"Postminimalism," The Aldrich Museum of Contemporary Art, Ridgefield, Connecticut
"Castelli and His Artists: Twenty-Five Years," Aspen Center for the Visual Arts, Colorado (traveled)
"Minimalism x 4," Whitney Museum of American Art, Downtown Branch, New York
"In Our Time," The Contemporary Arts Museum, Houston

1983 "1984—A Preview," Ronald Feldman Fine Arts, New York
"Twentieth Century Sculpture: Statements of Form," Whitney Museum of American Art, Midtown Branch, New York
"Twentieth Century Sculpture: Process and Presence," Whitney Museum of American Art, New York
"Beyond the Monument," Hayden Corridor Gallery, Massachusetts Institute of Technology, Cambridge
"Victims and Violations," Contemporary Arts Center, New Orleans
"New Art," Tate Gallery, London
"The End of the World: Contemporary Views of the Apocalypse," The New Museum, New York

1984 "The Shadow of the Bomb," University Gallery, University of Massachusetts, Amherst
"Ten Years of Collecting at the Museum of Contemporary Art," Museum of Contemporary Art, Chicago
"Endgame: Strategies of Postmodernist Performance," Hunter College Art Gallery, New York

"Dreams and Nightmares: Utopian Visions in Modern Art," Hirshhorn Museum and Sculpture Garden, Smithsonian Institution, Washington, D.C.
"Citywide Contemporary Sculpture Exhibition," The Toledo Museum of Art, Ohio
"American Sculpture," Margo Leavin Gallery, Los Angeles
"A Different Climate: Aspects of Beauty in Contemporary Art," Städtische Kunsthalle, Düsseldorf
"Content: A Contemporary Focus, 1974–1984," Hirshhorn Museum and Sculpture Garden, Smithsonian Institution, Washington, D.C.
"Rediscovered Romanticism," New Math Gallery, New York
"Group Exhibition," Sonnabend Gallery, New York
"Blam! The Explosion of Pop, Minimalism and Performance, 1958–1964," Whitney Museum of American Art, New York

1985 "Art Minimal I," CAPC Musée d'Art Contemporain, Bordeaux, France
"Minimal Art: A Survey of Early and Recent Work," John Weber Gallery, New York
"Citywide Contemporary Sculpture Exhibition," The Toledo Museum of Art, Ohio
"New Dimensions," Akron Art Museum, Ohio

SELECTED BIBLIOGRAPHY

Articles by the Artist

"Aligned with Nazca." *Artforum,* Vol. 14, October 1975, pp. 26–39, ill.

"American Quartet." *Art in America,* Vol. 69, December 1981, pp. 92–104, ill.

"Anti Form." *Artforum,* Vol. 6, April 1968, pp. 33–35, ill.

"The Art of Existence. Three Extra-Visual Artists: Work in Process." *Artforum,* Vol. 9, January 1971, pp. 28–33.

"Dance." *The Village Voice,* Part I: February 3, 1966, pp. 8, 24–25; Part II: February 10, p. 15.

"A Method for Sorting Cows." *Art and Literature,* Vol. 11, Winter 1967, p. 180.

"Notes on Sculpture." *Artforum,* Vol. 4, February 1966, pp. 42–44. (Reprinted in *Minimal Art,* ed. Gregory Battcock, New York: Dutton, 1968.)

"Notes on Sculpture, Part II." *Artforum,* Vol. 5, October 1966, pp. 20–23, ill. (Reprinted in *Minimal Art,* ed. Battcock.)

"Notes on Sculpture, Part III: Notes and Nonsequiturs." *Artforum,* Vol. 5, Summer 1967, pp. 24–29, ill.

"Notes on Sculpture, Part 4: Beyond Objects." *Artforum,* Vol. 7, April 1969, pp. 50–54, ill.

"Portfolio: 4 Sculptors." *Perspecta* (The Yale Architectural Journal), 1967, pp. 44–53.

"The Present Tense of Space." *Art in Amercia,* Vol. 66, January/February 1978, pp. 70–81, ill.

"Some Notes on the Phenomenology of Making: The Search for the Motivated." *Artforum,* Vol. 8, April 1970, pp. 62–66, ill.

"Some Splashes in the Ebb Tide." *Artforum,* Vol. 11, February 1973, pp. 42–49.

Published Interviews

With Jonathan Feinberg, in *Arts Magazine,* Vol. 55, September 1980.

With Achille Bonito Oliva, in *Domus,* Vol. 516, November 1972, pp. 43–44.

With L. Picard, in *Kunstwerk,* Vol. 25, March 1972, pp. 3–13.

"A Duologue," with David Sylvester, in *Robert Morris* (exhibition catalog), London: The Tate Gallery, 1971.

One-Person Exhibition Catalogs

Robert Morris. Eindhoven, Holland: Stedelijk van Abbemuseum, 1968. Essay by Jean Leering.

Robert Morris. Washington, D.C.: Corcoran Gallery of Art, 1969. Essay by Annette Michelson.

Robert Morris. New York: Whitney Museum of American Art, 1970. Essay by Marcia Tucker.

Robert Morris. London: The Bernie Press, 1971. Exhibition at the Tate Gallery.

Robert Morris. Saint Etienne, France: Musée d'Art et d'Industrie, 1974. Introduction by Bernard Ceysson.

Robert Morris: Mirror Works 1961–78. New York: Leo Castelli, Inc., 1979. Introduction by Robert Morris.

Robert Morris: Selected Works 1970–80. Houston: Contemporary Arts Museum, 1982. Essay by Marti Mayo.

Group Exhibition Catalogs and Books

American Drawings of the Sixties. New York: New School for Social Research Art Center, 1969. Introduction by Paul Mocsanyi.

American Sculpture of the 60s. Los Angeles: Los Angeles County Museum of Art, 1967. Ed. Maurice Tuchman.

Anti-Illusion: Procedures/Materials. New York: Whitney Museum of American Art, 1969. Essays by James Monte and Marcia Tucker.

The Art of the Real: U.S.A. 1948–1968. New York: Museum of Modern Art, 1968. Essay by E.C. Goossen.

Battcock, Gregory, ed. *Minimal Art, A Critical Anthology.* New York: Dutton, 1968.

Beardsley, John. *Probing the Earth; Contemporary Land Projects.* Washington, D.C.: Smithsonian Institution Press, 1977.

Chance and Art. Philadelphia: Institute of Contemporary Art, Pennsylvania University, 1970. Essay by Robert Pincus-Witten.

Der Raum in der Amerikanischen Kunst. Zurich: Kunsthaus, 1969. Introduction by Felix Andreas Bauman.

A Different Climate. Düsseldorf: Städtische Kunsthalle, 1984.

The Drawings of Robert Morris. Williamstown, Massachusetts: Williams College Museum of Art, 1982. Introduction by Thomas Krens.

Earth Art. Ithaca, New York: Andrew Dickson White Museum of Art, Cornell University, 1969.

Eight Sculptors: The Ambiguous Image. Minneapolis: Walker Art Center, 1966. Essay by Martin Friedman.

Endgame—Strategies of Postmodernist Performance. New York: Hunter College Art Gallery, 1984. Essay by Maurice Berger.

14 Sculptors: The Industrial Edge. Minneapolis: Walker Art Center, 1969. Essays by Barbara Rose and Christopher Finch.

Guggenheim International Exhibition 1967. New York: The Solomon R. Guggenheim Museum, 1967. Introduction by Edward F. Fry.

Joseph Kosuth—Robert Morris. Bradford, Massachusetts: Laura Knott Gallery, Bradford Junior College, 1969.

Large Drawings. Middletown, Connecticut: Ezra and Cecile Zilkha Gallery, Center for the Arts, Wesleyan University, 1984.

Lippard, Lucy R. *Overlay: Contemporary Art and the Art of Prehistory.* New York: Pantheon, 1983.

Minimal Art. Düsseldorf: Städtische Kunsthalle, 1969.

Mixed Media and Pop Art. Buffalo, New York: Albright-Knox Art Gallery/Buffalo Fine Arts Academy, 1963.

New York Painting & Sculpture 1940–1970. New York: Metropolitan Museum of Art, 1970.

New York 13. Vancouver, British Columbia: Vancouver Art Gallery, 1969. Essay by Lucy Lippard.

The Other Tradition. Philadelphia: Institute of Contemporary Art, Pennsylvania University, 1966. Essay by G.R. Swenson.

Plastics and the New Art. Philadelphia: Institute of Contemporary Art, Pennsylvania University, 1969. Essay by Stephen S. Prokopoff.

Primary Structures. New York: The Jewish Museum, The Jewish Theological Seminary of America, 1966. Introduction by Kynaston McShine.

Rose, Barbara. *American Art Since 1900.* New York and Washington: Praeger, 1967.

The Shadow of the Bomb. Mount Holyoke and Amherst, Massachusetts: Mount Holyoke College Art Museum and University Gallery, University of Massachusetts at Amherst, 1984. Essay by Sally Yard.

Soft Art. Trenton, New Jersey: New Jersey State Museum, 1969.

Victims and Violations. New York: Contemporary Arts Center, 1983.

When Attitudes Become Form. Bern, Switzerland: Kunsthalle, 1969. Essays by Harald Szeemann, Scott Burton, and Gregoire Müller.

Articles and Reviews

1965 Berrigan, Ted. "Reviews & Previews: Robert Morris." *Art News,* Vol. 63, February, p. 13.

Kozloff, Max. "The Further Adventures of American Sculpture." *Arts Magazine,* Vol. 39, February, pp. 24–31.

1966 Factor, Don. "Los Angeles—Robert Morris." *Artforum,* Vol. 4, May, p. 13.

Friedman, Martin. "Robert Morris: Polemics and Cubes." *Art International,* Vol. 10, December 20, pp. 23–27.

Lippard, Lucy R. "Rejective Art." *Art International,* Vol. 8, October 20, pp. 33–37.

Smithson, Robert. "Entropy and the New Monuments." *Artforum,* Vol. 4, June, pp. 26–31.

1967 Ashton, Dore. "Jeunes talents de la sculpture américaine." *Aujourd'hui,* Vol. 10, December 1966/January 1967, pp. 158–160.

Fried, Michael. "Art and Objecthood." *Artforum,* Vol. 5, January, pp. 30–31.

Lippard, Lucy R. "Eros Presumptive." *The Hudson Review,* Vol. 20, Spring, pp. 91–99.

Michelson, Annette. "10 x 10: 'concrete reasonableness.'" *Artforum,* Vol. 5, January, pp. 30–31.

Rainer, Yvonne. "Don't Give the Game Away." *Arts Magazine,* Vol. 41, April, pp. 44–47.

Rose, Barbara. "The Value of Didactic Art." *Artforum,* Vol. 5, April, pp. 32–36.

Rosenberg, Harold. "The Art World." *The New Yorker,* Vol. 43, February 25, pp. 99–109.

1968 Antin, David. "Differences—Sames: New York 1966–1967." *Metro,* No. 13, February, pp. 78–104.

Battcock, Gregory. "Robert Morris." *Arts Magazine,* Vol. 42, May, pp. 30–31.

Kaprow, Allan. "The Shape of the Art Environment." *Artforum,* Vol. 6, Summer, pp. 32–33.

Leering, J. "Robert Morris: 2 L-Shapes 1965." *Museumjournaal,* (Amsterdam: Rijksmuseum), Vol. 13, p. 135.

Leider, Philip. "The Properties of Materials: In the Shadow of Robert Morris." *The New York Times,* Section 2, December 22, p. 31D.

Rose, Barbara. "Blowup—The Problem of Scale in Sculpture." *Art in America.* Vol. 56, July/August, pp. 80–91.

Sauerwein, Laurent. "Two Sculptures by Robert Morris." *Studio International,* Vol. 175, May, p. 276.

Sharp, Willoughby. "Air Art." *Studio International,* Vol. 175, May, pp. 262–265.

1969 Kramer, Hilton. "The Emperor's New Bikini." *Art in America,* Vol. 57, January/February, pp. 48–55.

Müller, Gregoire. "Robert Morris Presents Anti-Form." *Arts Magazine,* Vol. 43, February, pp. 29–30.

Rose, Barbara. "Sculpture as an Intimate Art." *New York,* April 14, pp. 48–49.

Sharp, Willoughby. "Place and Process." *Artforum,* Vol. 8, November, pp. 46–49.

Shirey, David L. "Impossible Art—What It Is." *Art in America,* Vol. 57, May/June, pp. 32–47.

Wilson, William S. "Hard Questions and Soft Answers." *Art News,* Vol. 68, November, pp. 26–29, 81–84.

1970 Antin, David. "Lead Kindly Blight." *Art News,* Vol. 69, November, pp. 36–39, 87–90.

Burnham, Jack. "Robert Morris: Retrospective in Detroit." *Artforum,* Vol. 8, March, pp. 67–75.

Calas, Nicolas. "The Wit and Pedantry of Robert Morris." *Arts Magazine,* Vol. 44, March, pp. 44–47.

Goossen, E.C. "The Artist Speaks: Robert Morris." *Art in America,* Vol. 58, May, pp. 104–111.

Kramer, Hilton. "The Triumph of Ideas Over Art." *The New York Times,* Section 2, January 25, p. 27D.

1971 Celant, Germano. "Robert Morris: Information, documentation, archives." *Arte Contemporanea,* No. 7, pp. 36–43.

Reise, Barbara. "The Aborted Haacke and Robert Morris Shows." *Studio International,* Vol. 182, July, pp. 30–39.

1972 Burnham, Jack. "Voices from the Gate." *Arts Magazine,* Vol. 46, Summer, pp. 34–46.

Perrault, John. "A Sculpted Play on Words." *The Village Voice,* May 4, p. 30.

Schjeldahl, Peter. "Robert Morris: Maxi of the Minimals." *The New York Times,* Sunday, May 7.

1973 Krauss, Rosalind. "Sense and Sensibility." *Artforum,* Vol. 12, November, pp. 43–53.

1974 Fry, Edward F. "Robert Morris: The Dialectic." *Arts Magazine,* Vol. 49, September, pp. 22–24.

Gilbert-Rolfe, J. "Robert Morris: The Complication of Exhaustion." *Artforum,* Vol. 13, September, pp. 44–49.

Russell, John. "Felt Sculptures Dominate Robert Morris Exhibition." *The New York Times,* Saturday, April 20.

1975 Martin, Richard. "Persistent Sublime." *Arts Magazine,* Vol. 49, January, pp. 74–75.

1976 Tuchman, Phyllis. "American Art in Germany: The History of a Phenomenon." *Artforum,* Vol. 9, November, pp. 66–67.

1977 Kuspit, Donald B. "Authoritarian Abstraction." *Aesthetics,* Vol. 36, Fall, p. 27–28.

1978 Audette, Lawrence. "Robert Morris: Learning to See Again." *Ulster Arts,* Fall, pp. 8–10.

1979 Foote, Nancy. "Monument-Sculpture-Earthwork." *Artforum,* Vol. 18, October, pp. 32–37.

Ratcliff, Carter. "Robert Morris: Prisoner of Modernism." *Art in America,* Vol. 67, October, pp. 96–109.

1980 Clay, Grady. "Reports: Earthworks Move Upstage." *Landscape Architecture,* Vol. 70, January, pp. 55–57.

Eisenman, Stephen F. "The Space of the Self: Robert Morris in the Realm of the Carceral." *Arts Magazine,* Vol. 55, September, pp. 104–109.

Kuspit, Donald B. "The Artist (Neo-Dandy) Stripped Bare by his Critic (Neo-Careerist), Almost." *Arts Magazine,* Vol. 54, May, pp. 134–137.

Meyer, Michael R. "Vito Acconci, Robert Morris, Dennis Oppenheim." *ArtWorld,* March 19.

Morgan, Stuart. "Vito Acconci, Robert Morris, Dennis Oppenheim—Sonnabend Gallery." *Artforum,* Vol. 18, Summer, pp. 82–33.

Pieszak, Devonna. "Robert Morris." *The New Art Examiner* (Chicago), July, p. 17.

Staniszewski, Mary Anne. "Acconci, Morris, Oppenheim." *Artnews,* Vol. 79, September, p. 248.

Zito, Abby. "New Concepts in Environmental Sculpture." *Art Speak,* March 27, p. 6.

1981 Crossley, Mimi. "Art: Robert Morris: Selected Works 1970–80." *The Houston Post,* Sunday, December 20.

Gintz, Claude. "Du Minimalisme au Néo-Baroque." *Artistes,* March/April, No. 8.

Johnson, Patricia C. "The Total Experience of Robert Morris." *Houston Chronicle,* Sunday, December 20.

Swift, Mary. "Metaphor: New Projects by Contemporary Sculptors." *Art in America,* Vol. 69, December.

1982 Flood, Richard. "Purchase." *Artforum,* Vol. 20, May, p. 88.

Kalil, Susie. "Robert Morris: Provocative Visual Vocabularies." *Artweek,* Vol. 13, February 13, p. 1.

————. "Robert Morris." *Artnews,* Vol. 81, May, p. 149.

Linker, Kate. "Metaphor: New Projects by Contemporary Sculptors." *Artforum,* Vol. 20, March, pp. 72–73.

1983 Adcock, Craig. "The Big Bad: A Critical Comparison of Mount Rushmore and Modern Earthworks." *Arts Magazine,* Vol. 57, April, pp. 104–107.

Cohen, Ronny. "Robert Morris." *Artnews,* Vol. 82, March, p. 159.

Lichtenstein, Therese. "Robert Morris." *Arts Magazine,* Vol. 57, March, pp. 40–41.

————. "A Tomb Outside the City." *The Village Voice,* February 1, p. 67.

————. "Robert Morris." *The New York Times,* January 28.

McGreevy, Linda F. "Robert Morris' Metaphorical Nightmare: The Jornada del Muerto." *Arts Magazine,* Vol. 58, September, pp. 107–109.

Marmer, Nancy. "Death in Black and White." *Art in America,* Vol. 71, March, p. 129–133.

Patton, Phil. "Robert Morris and the Fire Next Time." *Artnews,* Vol. 82, December, pp. 84–91.

Renard, Delphine. "Robert Morris (at Galerie Daniel Templon)." *Art Press* (Expositions), July/August.

1984 Gablik, Suzi. "Art Alarms: Visions of the End." *Art in America,* Vol. 72, April. p. 11. (Cover illustration.)

Howell, John. "Endgame." *Artforum,* Vol. 23, November, p. 101.

Russell, John. "Good Art Knows When To Shut Up." *The New York Times,* Sunday, November 25.

1985 Glueck, Grace. "Robert Morris." *The New York Times,* January 18.

Larson, Kay. "Robert Morris Goes Baroque." *New York Magazine,* January 28.

Levin, Kim. "Apocalyptic Paint." *The Village Voice,* January 29.

Ratcliff, Carter. "Robert Morris: A Saint Jerome for our times." *Artforum,* Vol. 23, April, pp. 60–63.

MUSEUM COLLECTIONS

Allen Memorial Art Museum, Oberlin College, Ohio
Dallas Museum of Fine Arts
The Detroit Institute of Arts
Milwaukee Art Center
Moderna Museet, Stockholm
The Museum of Modern Art, New York
National Gallery of Canada, Ottawa
National Gallery of Victoria, Melbourne, Australia
Pasadena Art Museum, California
The Tate Gallery, London
Wadsworth Atheneum, Hartford, Connecticut
Walker Arts Center, Minneapolis
Whitney Museum of American Art, New York

Lenders to the Exhibition

Leo Castelli Gallery, New York
Mr. Asher B. Edelman, New York
Gerald S. Elliott, Chicago
Sherry Fabrikant, New York
Suzanne and Howard Feldman, New York
Robert and Nancy Kaye, New York
Pamela and James Heller, New York
Robert Morris, New York
Private Collection, New York, courtesy of Sonnabend Gallery, New York
The Rivendell Collection, New York
Estelle Schwartz, New York courtesy Sonnabend Gallery, New York
Martin Sklar, New York
Sonnabend Gallery, New York

Acknowledgments

In January 1985 the Sonnabend Gallery and Castelli Gallery in New York held joint exhibitions of recent works by Robert Morris. Independently we saw the exhibition, were moved by Morris's most recent works, and expressed an interest in organizing a show that would include the recent works as well as earlier works from the 1980s. It was natural, then, that the Museum of Contemporary Art and the Newport Harbor Art Museum would collaborate in the organization of an exhibition of Robert Morris's works of the eighties. The successful accomplishment of this project in the brief interim time span was made possible by the generous cooperation and concerned dedication of a number of individuals.

Robert Morris is gratefully acknowledged for his support of the project from its inception, for his willingness to encourage the organization of an exhibition of large-scale, very delicate works and, most importantly, for the works themselves and the insights he provided for us in interpreting them. Ileana Sonnabend and Antonio Homem of the Sonnabend Gallery have been extremely generous in all aspects of the organization of this exhibition. We are also grateful for the cooperation of Stefano Basilico, Michael Fliegler, and Nicholas Scheidy of Sonnabend Gallery. Leo Castelli of the Leo Castelli Gallery has been of great assistance in organizing this exhibition as have Patty Brundage, Mary Jo Marks and Lisa Martizia of his staff.

The many lenders to the exhibition are acknowledged for allowing these important and, for the most part, recently acquired works to travel. Their commitment to the artist, his work, and this exhibition has been magnanimous. The exhibition has been greatly enhanced by the contributions of two art historians, Donald Kuspit and Edward Fry. Their unique and divergent insights into the artist and his work will assuredly enhance the understanding of Morris's art in the eighties and its relationship to his oeuvre. The catalog represents the contributions of many other individuals as well: Sue Henger, editor at Newport Harbor Art Museum, has coordinated all aspects of compilation, editing and printing. Michael Danoff's contribution of text to the plates section of the catalog is sincerely appreciated, and catalog designer Lilli Cristin is acknowledged for her accomplished and sensitive design.

On the Museum of Contemporary Art staff, thanks are due to Curatorial Assistant Mary Anne Wolff for her coordination of loans and assistance with the production of the catalog. Our gratitude also goes to Terry Ann R. Neff, Publications Coordinator, who reviewed the catalog copy for the Museum of Contemporary Art. Lela Hersh, Registrar, organized all shipping and insurance arrangements for the tour, and the efforts of Preparators Geoffrey Grove and Ian Edwards enabled the Museum to realize the installation of this exhibition. Special thanks go to Director I. Michael Danoff, whose long-standing interest and research into the artist's work made him an informed and supportive collaborator in bringing about this exhibition in Chicago. In addition, the Board of Trustees under President Helyn D. Goldenberg and the Exhibition Committee guided by Chairman William J. Hokin continue to enable the Museum of Contemporary Art to present such challenging and timely exhibitions of recent art.

On the Newport Harbor Art Museum staff, thanks are due to Natasha E.K. Sigmund for her capable assistance in the registration aspects of the exhibition. Efforts of the Operations and Preparator staff of the Museum are acknowledged, particularly the assistance of Richard Tellinghuisen and Brian Gray, who supervised the installation operation. Margie Shackelford, Director of Development, is recognized for her fund-raising efforts on behalf of the exhibition. Director Kevin Consey has been supportive of this project from the outset, as has the Program Committee of the Newport Harbor Art Museum chaired by Pamela Goldstein (past) and Leon Lyon (present).

The organization of this exhibition has been handled professionally and amicably by two institutions that had never previously worked together. This kind of collaboration on significant contemporary art exhibitions is always instrumental in bringing the best new work to a wider public.

Mary Jane Jacob, Chief Curator
Museum of Contemporary Art

Paul Schimmel, Chief Curator
Newport Harbor Art Museum

Photography Credits

Jon Abbott, New York: pages 4, 11, 12, 25, 27, 29, 31, 33 (right), 35, 37, 39, 49, 51, 53, 57, 59, 61
Bevan Davies, New York: page 20
Ursula Edelmann, Frankfurt, West Germany: page 33 (left)
Leo Castelli Gallery, New York: pages 18, 43, 46
Dorothy Zeidman, New York: pages 45, 63
Zindman/Fremont, New York: page 41

All photographs courtesy of Leo Castelli Gallery, New York

Robert Morris: Works of the Eighties
was produced by the MUSEUM OF
CONTEMPORARY ART, Chicago, Illinois
and the NEWPORT HARBOR ART
MUSEUM, Newport Beach, California
Edited by Sue Henger
Designed by Lilli Cristin
Typeset in Futura Medium and Times Roman
by Orange County Typesetting
Manufactured in Japan by Dai Nippon Printing
Company in an edition of 2,500 copies